THE OPEN UNIVERSITY

Social Sciences: a third level course
Research Methods in Education and
the Social Sciences

Block 6   Making Sense of Data

DE304 Research Methods in Education and the Social Sciences

Central Course Team
Michael Wilson (Chairman)
John Bynner
    (Chairman, Production)
Judith Calder
Peter Coxhead
Jeff Evans (on secondment
    from Middlesex Polytechnic)
Martyn Hammersley
Jane Henry (IET)
Fred Lockwood (IET)
Robert Peacock
Roger Sapsford
Keith Stribley (Course Assistant)
Betty Swift
Melanie Bayley (Editor)
Giles Clark (Editor)
Aldwyn Cooper (SCS)
Peter Cox (SCS)
Martyn Haywood (SCS)
Vic Lockwood (BBC)
Ken Patton (BBC)
Tag Taylor (Designer)
Eleanor Thompson (Project Control)

External Assessor
Marie Jahoda CBE
(Emeritus Professor of Social
Psychology, University of Sussex)

Internal Consultants
Christopher Brook
Michael Drake
Judith Greene
Andrew Pollard
Adrian Thomas

External Consultants
Liz Atkins, Medical Research Council
Paul Atkinson, University College, Cardiff
Martin Bulmer, London School of Economics
Wyn Lewis, University of Warwick
Cathie Marsh, University of Cambridge
Peter Martin, University of Manchester
Desmond Nuttall, Middlesex Examining Board
Bram Oppenheim, London School of Economics
Albert Pilliner, University of Edinburgh
David Romney, Laurentian University, Ontario

Acknowledgements

The Course Team are indebted to the following for their assistance: John Murrell and John Bibby for their comments on the draft material; Patrick Miller for preparing the Glossary; David Short and the students who developmentally tested the course; Professor Jim Davis for invaluable help with the survey analysis section; Paul Smith for preparing the course library guide; Michael Levers and Tim Chard for photographic work; Keith Howard for graphic illustrations; Liz Joseph, Cathy Bayntun, Mary Cox, Betty Gregory and Ann Boomer, who were the course secretaries; Pat Coombes and Glenna White who helped with the preparation of drafts for publishing. Many others, both from the Open University and elsewhere, have helped to realize this course — to them our thanks.

The Open University Press
Walton Hall, Milton Keynes
MK7 6AA

First published 1979. Reprinted 1981, 1986.

Copyright © 1979 The Open University

Designed by the Graphic Design Group of the Open University.

Printed in Great Britain by Staples Printers St Albans Limited at The Priory Press.

ISBN 0 335 07441 3

This text forms part of an Open University course. The complete list of the course appears at the end of this text.

For general availability of supporting material referred to in this text, please write to Open University Educational Enterprises Limited, 12 Cofferidge Close, Stony Stratford, Milton Keynes, MK11 1BY, Great Britain.

Further information on Open University courses may be obtained from the Admissions Office, The Open University, P.O. Box 48, Walton Hall, Milton Keynes, MK7 6AB.

Introduction to Block 6

Blocks 2 to 5 of the course have shown you (a) how to frame an hypothesis so that it may be tested, (b) how to design a research project which satisfies your research aims, (c) how to design and test instruments for data collection, (d) how to extract, code, and perhaps simplify your data, and (e) how to enter the field and collect data in the ethnographic style. Block 6 now shows you how you make sense of the data which you have collected.

'To make sense of' in this context means to find patterns in your data which are interesting and which bear upon your (or another researcher's) research questions. These patterns may enable you to construct explanations and models of the way in which the particular aspect of the world explored operates. The first problem, then, is how does one look for these patterns: what are the ways of analysing data to find them? Here the research styles diverge from each other and the techniques used depend very much on the style in which one is working.

At this stage in the research process in survey analysis one would have a *data matrix*, i.e. information collected about n individuals (respondents, organizations, schools, etc.) each of which has an observation recorded on each of m variables. You can think of the data matrix as a table (usually a large one) with n rows, each of which corresponds to an individual, and m columns, each of which corresponds to a variable. You met data matrices in Block 2 and below is an example.

An example of a data matrix

Variable	1	2	3	. . . *m*
Respondent	Age code	Party identity	Social class	
1	5	1	7	. . .
2	4	7	3	. . .
3	5	5	3	. . .
4	3	3	1	. . .
5	2	3	4	. . .
6	5	7	5	. . .
.	.	.	.	
.	.	.	.	etc.
.	.	.	.	
n				

Note   The variables are shown with their coded values
Source: Oxford Social Mobility Survey, 1974 (extract)

This is our starting point in survey analysis. We analyse our data by taking hypotheses such as 'Increasing age leads to increasing identification with the Conservative Party' and seeing whether they are supported by the pattern of the data in our survey. In short we would see if 'age' and 'Conservative identity' are positively associated or correlated. How to do this is discussed in Part 2 ('Two Variable Analysis') and in Part 3 ('Hypothesis Testing').

There remain, however, many problems with the analysis of survey data, problems which require a series of decisions to be taken about how to treat the data. You will often find, for example, that some observations are missing from the matrix; what to do about this problem is answered in Part 2. Alternatively, it may be desirable (and often necessary) to reduce the amount of information in your matrix in order to make analysis feasible. In the example I have just given, social class is coded on a seven-point scale, running from the higher professionals and managers of large enterprises to semi- and unskilled workers. This information may well be too detailed to use in the analysis and the simpler distinction between 'manual' and 'non-manual' may serve better. In Cathie Marsh's words (the author of Part 2), tables are often 'storehouses of information'. The task of the analyst is to make that storehouse 'tell a story'. Moreover, the story you tell has to be justified on the evidence of your data.

Part 2, then, deals with tabulated data which come primarily from surveys. Experimental data can also be analysed by the techniques expounded by Cathie Marsh. In fact, the problem of *causal inference* is really only soluble by the experimental manipulation of the independent variable. The ability to manipulate the independent variable is rare for the reasons indicated in Part 2 and mentioned as early as Block 1, Part 1. Experimenters do not usually analyse their data through the use of simple cross-tabulation of variables, although there is no good reason why they should not. Partly because the experimental dependent variable is normally of an interval level of measurement more powerful techniques than those of Part 2 can be used, including the analysis of variance (known as ANOVA by abbreviation) and multiple regression (known as MR). Block 7 deals with MR and ANOVA in the context of analysis using the general linear model. Part 2 of this Block, however, gives you a simpler method for the analysis of data than Block 7, taking two variables at a time. The methods which are demonstrated are limited to quantitative data and are appropriate for calculation by hand or (much better) by pocket calculator without the need for sophisticated mathematics. 'Elementary survey analysis', as the techniques of Part 2 are sometimes known, relies on collapsing the categories of any variable to two values or on using data which are dichotomous anyway. As higher levels of measurement can always be degraded to a dichotomy, the techniques of Part 2 are of universal applicability. The 'two-by-two' tables used are one type of *contingency table*, the general name for the cross-tabulation of one variable against one or more other variables. When we inspect the entries in such a table we look to see if the values of one variable are contingent (or conditional) on the values of the other variable. One can, in principle, look for contingent associations between several variables at the same time but this is beyond the scope of an undergraduate course.

The analysis of tabular data in contingency tables is probably the method which most of you will prefer to use in order to analyse your Survey Project data. Many of the variables on which you collect information will be either nominal (such as sex) or ordinal (such as social class) which are easier to tackle using the methods of Block 6, Parts 2 and 3. You *can* analyse your Survey Project data using regression techniques (as in Block 7, Parts 1 and 2) and some of you may wish to do so, but you would need to use dummy variables.

One problem that you will meet in analysing your project data is the possibility that third variables are implicated in the associations which you may find in your two variable analysis. Normally, a researcher would have to control for the possible effects of a third variable on a two variable relationship which was being inspected. The Appendix to Part 2 shows you some simple techniques for calculating the partial associations amongst three variables and for measuring interaction effects.

Finding and measuring patterns of association in your data are the first steps in making sense of them. You will, however, be directed by theoretical and substantive issues in your search as well as by statistical requirements. Your ultimate goal is the construction of an explanation of why (for example) older age is positively associated with greater identification with the Conservative Party. This is where the real difficulties lie since no single research project is likely to be conclusive on any problem. Still, you should try to be as definite as you can on the conclusions which you draw, even if you recognize them to be less than satisfactory because of the uncertainties involved.

One uncertainty you will face (in common with all reported research) is the decision to accept or reject an hypothesis. To cross-tabulate age and party identity as two variables from a larger data matrix is to test the hypothesis that age and Conservative Party identity are related. Say you obtain a coefficient of association of +0.26 (which you may think of as just like a correlation coefficient with a minimum of 0 and maxima of ± 1), what can you conclude after this analysis? When you know that the association is based on the evidence from 106 cases, you may suspect that your observed association is a chance sampling fluctuation and that other samples from the same population may show a zero association. You would be right to be suspicious but you can, after testing, decide if you are well-advised to accept or to reject your hypothesis.

Part 3 of this Block, 'Hypothesis Testing', lays down the guidelines covering how to take a decision on whether to accept or reject an hypothesis on the available data. Since survey analysis rests on samples drawn randomly from populations it is possible to use the laws of probability to say whether an hypothesis is likely or not to be acceptable for the parent population. Similarly, a well-designed experiment will randomly allocate individuals to different 'treatments', so that, again by using the laws of probability, we can decide whether or not the patterns observed are likely to have arisen by chance.

Thus under conditions of random selection of samples or of random allocation of individuals to groups, we can take probability decisions on the testing of hypotheses. The methods outlined in Part 3, therefore, are applicable to data in both the experimental and survey styles, but are not applicable to the analysis of ethnographic data. Let us briefly review the reasons why this is so.

Ethnography is an intensive methodology; that is, it elicits and analyses a great deal of data from a very few respondents or from only one 'setting'. Surveys and experiments, on the other hand, are much more extensive in their methods; less information is elicited from (relatively) many respondents. Now, the laws of probability on which statistical testing is based only give us useful results when large numbers are involved. The ethnographer will be limited to one or a few individuals or settings and can never be sure that the one (or few) chosen is typical of the population which it represents. In contrast, surveys will usually draw large numbers of respondents by random means from a defined population and can, therefore, be confident (within knowable limits, as Parts 2 and 3 of this Block show) of the sample representing the population. (A sample of one or of a few will only be representative of a wider group if the individuals do not differ from one another on any relevant characteristic.) Ethnographers are aware of this problem but find it difficult to solve because of their concern with the problems of naturalism and understanding and because of the intensive, time-consuming nature of field-work which results from this concern.

How ethnographers draw conclusions from their data and construct explanations will be discussed in Part 1, but note at this point that their aim is explanation which applies to many cases (as opposed to the specific explanation of a unique event) and this is something they share with the other styles of research. Ethnographers, too, use hypotheses but they do not test them by the use of experiments or surveys. In short, ethnographers have the same goals as other social scientists but try to reach them by other means.[1]

'By other means' implies a different procedure. Hypotheses in ethnography are not, as they are in surveys and experiments, conjectures about relationships in

[1] *While this is the view presented in this course, not all ethnographers would agree with it.*

which the concepts are strictly operationalized and in which the data collected have a degree of structuring which enables quantification and hence statistical testing to take place. The ethnographer must first establish what concepts the actors in his chosen setting use to make sense of their world. He progressively focuses his attention on what is to be explained and only arrives at a recognizable hypothesis quite late in his research. Much ethnography goes no further than this since the researcher has already travelled a long road to reach his hypotheses or theory. For this reason descriptive exploratory studies of new fields of investigation are common in ethnography and the problems defined and explanations offered stem only from a single case; Ball (1972; set reading in Block 1) is such an example.

If the ethnographer is able and willing to go further than arriving at a set of hypotheses or a theory then, in principle, he can test it; but the procedures are not those of statistical testing. He would use *analytic induction*, a process whereby the hypotheses are tried in other settings in an attempt to find negative instances. This is indeed a rigorous form of testing, just as much as statistical tests based on quantified data. In many cases analytic induction is *more* rigorous because it employs naturalistic case studies and, compared to surveys or experiments, the ethnographic study faces the problem of ecological validity better than does most research in the other styles.

'Making sense of data' in the final sense must mean arriving at explanations which have withstood testing, the more rigorous the testing the better. In this way there is an underlying unity of the three styles; though the procedures for constructing and testing explanations may differ between the styles, they should conform to one fundamental logic of science whether their data is qualitative or quantitative. Although in ethnography it is more time-consuming to test explanations than to do so in surveys or experiments, analytic induction provides a suitable method to match the statistical tests of Part 3.

The Structure of Block 6

Part 1: Analysing Ethnographic Data   This Part covers the process of analysis from interpreting and coding the data records to advancing explanations of problems. It is self-contained, unlike Parts 2 and 3, in that it deals with analysis right up to forms of publication. As this introduction has already made clear ethnography follows different methods in constructing and testing its explanations and therefore it requires separate treatment in this course.

Part 2: Two Variable Analysis   Part 2 deals with the analysis of quantified data presented in tabular form stemming mainly from the survey style but also useful for experimental data. The main aim of Part 2 is to introduce methods of simplifying tabular data for two variables to the point where a single figure can summarize the information contained in a table (a measure of association for dichotomized variables). This Part then concludes by taking account of the fact that the data in a table nearly always come from a sample and that our measure of association in the population (based on the sample) is subject to varying degrees of confidence in its accuracy.

The Appendix to Part 2: Introducing a Third Variable   This briefly shows what effect a third variable may have on a two variable association and uses the concepts of partial correlation and interaction.

Part 3: Hypothesis Testing   This is an extension of Part 2. It deals with the idea that any association observed in tabular data may be framed as an hypothesis and subjected to testing. The rejection or acceptance of an hypothesis is a form of statistical decision which depends on the level of measurement of the variables and on the size of the risks which the analyst decides to take when he may wrongly reject an hypothesis or wrongly accept it. Hypothesis testing is equally relevant to both the survey and experimental styles.

Relationship of Block 6 to the Course as a Whole

Part 1 is the final exposition of ethnographic methods in the course and follows on from Block 3, Part 5 and Block 4, Part 3.

Part 2 is a thorough treatment of the analysis of tables begun in Block 2, Part 4. It does not require any new statistics other than d, which is related to the Phi coefficient ($\emptyset$) which you met briefly in Block 2. The estimation of a confidence interval for d is similiar to the estimation of population statistics from samples, which you met in Block 3, Part 4, 'Introduction to Applied Sampling'.

Part 3 on hypothesis testing begins by taking a related approach to the estimation of confidence intervals in Part 2, that of significance testing. If you understand confidence intervals you will find it easier to grasp the idea of a significance test. This Part introduces you to statistics which you have not met before, namely the z, χ^2, and t statistics. You will meet t again in Block 7, Part 1.

Block 7 (Parts 1 and 2) parallels Block 6, Part 2. The general linear model in Block 7 is of wider applicability than the tabular analysis of data in Block 6 but we think that you will find the statistical ideas in it more difficult to apply than those in Block 6, Part 2, though not more difficult to understand. The general linear model can be used for both interval and nominal data but the methods of Block 6 may only be used on nominal data. Since data can be degraded in a downward direction, analysis of nominal data is always possible but sometimes at the price of the loss of information. You will find Block 7 much easier to understand if you first work carefully through Block 6, Parts 2 and 3. Part 3, 'Hypothesis Testing', is essential for Block 7.

Aims of Block 6

Block 6 has the aim of showing how data which you or a researcher have collected may be analysed so that you may draw conclusions and perhaps state them with a known confidence in their validity. The second aim (which follows from the first) is that of evaluating the conclusions which are drawn in research reports from data presented as evidence by a researcher.

Study Guide for Block 6

Parts 2 and 3 should be studied in the order in which they occur, since Part 3 on hypothesis testing is based on the discussion of two variable analysis in Part 3.

Part 1 may be studied before or after Parts 2 and 3 since it comprises a separate treatment of the analysis of ethnographic data; Parts 2 and 3 are applicable only to data derived from the survey and experimental styles.

In the guide to the course we have suggested a study time budget for each Part: the real limit to study time, however, is the total for the Block; within that, different students will undoubtedly want to devote different amounts of time to each of the Parts.

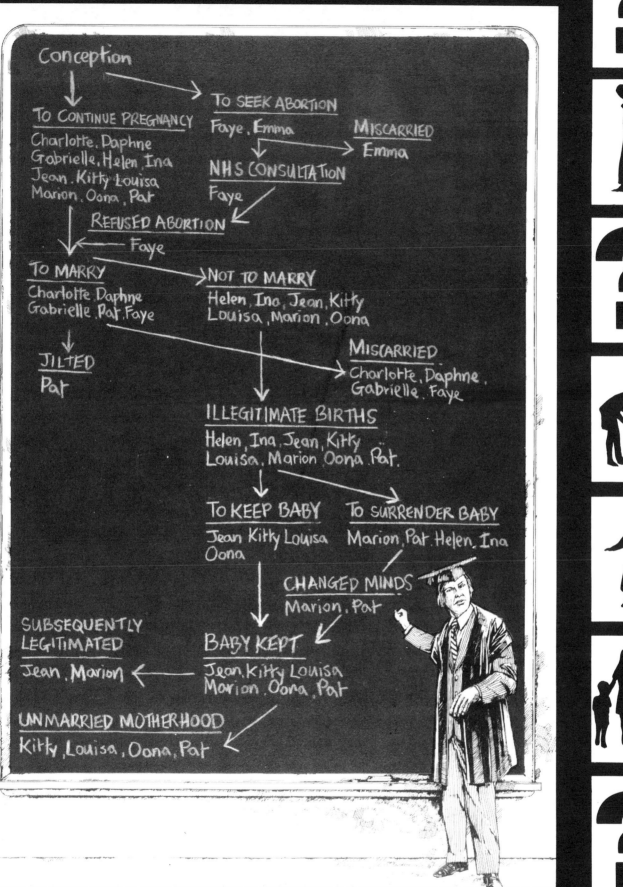

Part 1   Analysing Ethnographic Data
Prepared by Martyn Hammersley for the Course Team

Block 6   Part 1

Contents

Aims

To develop the conception of explanation usually associated with ethnographic research, to outline various principles and strategies involved in the generation and testing of theory within this style and to discuss issues arising in the writing up and publication of research reports.

Study Guide

You will find indications in the text of the appropriate points at which to read the set material. There are a number of ITQs, SAQs and Activities which I hope you will find useful. My own answers to these are given at the end of the Part.

Set Reading

CRESSEY, D. R. (1950) 'The criminal violation of financial trust', supplied as Supplementary Material.

BECKER, H. S. (1964) 'Problems in the publication of field studies', in Bynner, J. and Stribley, K. M. (eds) (1979) Ch. 24.

SUDNOW, D. (1965) 'Normal crimes: sociological features of the penal code in a Public Defender Office', supplied as Supplementary Material.

Recommended Reading

BECKER, H. S. (1958) 'Problems of inference and proof in participant observation', in Bynner, J. and Stribley, K. M. (eds) (1979) Ch. 23.

DENZIN, N. K. (1971) 'The logic of naturalistic inquiry', in Bynner, J. and Stribley, K. M. (eds) (1979) Ch. 5.

WISEMAN, J. (1974) 'The research web', in Bynner, J. and Stribley, K. M. (eds) (1979) Ch. 10.

VON WRIGHT, G. H. (1971) 'Two traditions', in Bynner, J. and Stribley, K. M. (eds) (1979) Ch. 2.

Further Reading

DENZIN, N. K. (1970) *The research act*, London, Butterworths.

GLASER, B. and STRAUSS, A. (1968) *The discovery of grounded theory*, London, Weidenfeld and Nicolson.

LOFLAND, J. (1971) *Analyzing Social Settings*, London, Wadsworth.

SCHATZMAN, L. and STRAUSS, A. (1968) *Field research*, London, Prentice-Hall.

1   The Nature of Ethnographic Analysis

1.1   We have stressed throughout this course that the differences between the three research traditions arise from differential emphasis on certain common methodological problems and from the adoption of different strategies for dealing with these. In the area of data analysis the primacy of the problems of description for ethnographers has meant that they have made little use of statistical analysis. As I noted in Block 4, Part 3, there is a dilemma here. The methods which ethnographers use to counter the threats to validity, which I summarized under the headings of discovery, understanding, multiple perspectives and naturalism, actually worsen the problems of control and representation. On the other hand, the methods adopted by researchers in the experimental and survey traditions to achieve control and representation increase the dangers of misunderstanding, procedural reactivity and so on. There is no easy answer to this problem but we shall examine one possible solution, the combination of methods, in Block 8. In this Part I shall be concerned solely with the analytic methods currently employed by ethnographers; or rather with what I consider to be the central ones, since the range of such methods is quite diverse, reflecting in part a diversity of theoretical orientation.

1.2   In Block 1 two different approaches to the explanation of social phenomena were discussed.

Outline the major differences between these two approaches.

Covering laws.
Explanatic by understanding.

1.3   One involved appeal to covering-laws, the work of Jenkins and Macrae (1967) on the relationship between inter-community communication and conflict providing an example. The other approach was termed explanation-by-understanding, and involved reference to intentions, motives and social rules, in short to social meanings. What is at issue here is whether human actions can be explained without reference to reasons, motives, etc., that is, without reference to social meanings.

Block 1, Part 3, section 8

1.4   Ethnographers generally argue that this is not possible. However, they do not usually deny the importance of remote causal relationships. Most people working in the ethnographic tradition seem to take the view, in practice at least, that explanations can and should employ both reasons and causes. For example, in the sociology of deviance, ethnographers have certainly placed great emphasis on the perspectives and cultures of deviant actors. But they also accord significance to the situation faced by these actors in the development of those perspectives and cultures. In particular, it has been suggested that being publicly labelled and treated as deviant, being prosecuted and placed in a prison or mental hospital for example, changes the personal circumstances and sense of self of actors in such a way as to shape their future behaviour: the labelling of deviants often results in an increase in their deviant activities (Rubington and Weinberg, 1968). In analysing data from participation, observation, interviews and documents, therefore, the ethnographer is normally concerned both with exploring and describing intentions, motives, perspectives and cultures *and* with developing theories regarding how these social meanings relate to the situations faced by the actors concerned. Indeed, he often goes beyond this, seeking more general models of the way in which these situations fit into the larger social structure: how they themselves have been produced.

1.5   What distinguishes ethnographic analysis from most work in the other two traditions is a greater emphasis on the importance of linking the researcher's own *analytic concepts* with the terms in which the actors themselves understand their situations and actions. An example may help here. Much research on social class has been concerned with documenting the hierarchy of social classes in industrial societies. Researchers in this area generally begin with a set of occupational titles, often inherited with minor modifications from previous studies, then ask a large sample of respondents to rank these titles in descending order of status.

analytic concept

On what grounds do you think an ethnographer might criticize this technique?

Respondent may not have systematic idea of class. If has, may not coincide with interviewers

---

1.6   Such an approach makes a number of assumptions which most ethnographers would take to be fruitful topics of investigation in themselves; for example:

(a)   that social status considerations are a salient aspect of people's lives; that these are a major feature of the way in which they categorize and act towards others in everyday life.

(b)   that people have a single, context-free notion of social status rather than a number of different notions which they treat as relevant in different circumstances. A special case of this is the assumption that the ranking elicited in the survey has implications for people's actions in their everyday life and in particular for those attitudes and actions of concern to the researchers: for example, occupational aspirations and mobility strategies.

(c)   that if social status is a primary orientation in everyday life and if there is only one ranking, the occupational titles provided are the terms in which people think of social status. In fact, one of the reasons survey researchers generally provide respondents with a list of occupational titles rather than asking them to use their own terms is because of the incredible variety of occupational designations.

(d)   that people conceptualize social status in hierarchical, rather than, for instance, dichotomous or even horizontal terms.

1.7   Of course, I am certainly not suggesting that it is impossible for survey researchers to consider such issues. My point is simply that these issues have been neglected in much research on occupational prestige and social mobility. For those in the ethnographic tradition, on the other hand, with their emphasis on the problems of description, these kinds of issues are primary. This does have its costs, however, in that it is much more difficult for ethnographers to produce accounts of national occupational prestige and social mobility patterns. The ethnographer reluctantly accepts these costs in the hope that they may not be permanent. We are faced with a dilemma of which there is no easy resolution.

1.8   The ethnographer begins his analysis by trying to describe the perspectives and actions of the actors involved in the scene he is studying. He seeks to build his concepts on those of participants in such a way that they incorporate and explain those social meanings.

SAQ 1

How might an ethnographer set about investigating the nature and the role of social status in modern societies?

Spend ten minutes answering this question.

1.9   In studying social status the ethnographer could investigate various settings so as to provide a basis for describing those aspects of people's perspectives concerned with status. But this would only be the beginning of his analysis. Even if he were to discover that status considerations play no role at all in people's categorizations of and actions towards others, this would not necessarily render the concept of status group or social class analytically useless. He might be able to show that by such categorizations people nevertheless unwittingly differentiate others in ways which reflect the others' membership of particular status groups or social classes. Thus, for example, while court personnel may not explicitly orient to others in status terms, legal process may still result in very different outcomes for members of different status groups, or social classes, even where the offence involved is substantially the same. Alternatively, the ethnographer may be able to show that the way in which a particular group of people categorize others derives from that group's social class position. The important point is that the ethnographer begins by analysing the perspectives of participants, the social meanings embedded in action, even though he eventually develops analytic concepts which go beyond those meanings. There is no way of moving straight to analytic concepts, by-passing social meanings, because the latter play a crucial role in generating the patterns of social action which we as social scientists are seeking to explain.

1.10   *Summary*   Ethnographers are concerned with both reasons and causes. However, much more than those in the other traditions, they stress the importance of beginning the analysis with the description of actors' perspectives and they emphasize the problems involved in developing descriptions of perspectives, actions and settings. At present this generally results in a failure to produce data which are open to statistical analysis and this makes the problems of representation and control more difficult. However, as we shall see, this does not mean that the generation and testing of social theory in ethnography is impossible.

2   The Process of Analysis: Segmenting and Filing the Data

2.1   Very soon after the beginning of the data collection process the researcher is faced with the problem of a gradually mounting body of documents, field-notes from participant observation and interviews, and perhaps also transcripts. He has to begin to file this material.

How do you think such data records could be most usefully filed?

In 'category' headings once such things begin to emerg.

2.2   The most obvious kind of filing system is a *running record* by time of collection; this is the basic file used by the ethnographer. In itself, though, it is not sufficient; it is also necessary to begin to file data according to its relevance to the categories that are emerging from the analysis. The running record still remains a crucial resource, however, since it allows any piece of data to be examined in the context in which it emerged.

running record

2.3   The first step in analysis is to *segment the data*. Often there are 'natural' breaks in the material which can be used to break it up into chunks that can then be allocated to particular categories. This is usually the case with participant observation field-notes which often consist of notes on a sequence of incidents, each of which can be treated as a separate segment. However, sometimes the 'natural' breaks are so few and far between that, simply for practical purposes, the data must be broken up in a more artificial way.

segmentation of data

2.4   Each data segment is then analysed, a process which I shall discuss in the next two sections, and allocated to one or more categories, either by being physically placed in a pile of data relevant to that particular category or by the use of punched cards or some other system.

2.5   Some of the categories used will be substantive, for example relating to particular persons or sites, others will be theoretical, concerned with particular types or aspects of social process. The filing of data records will, in line with the discovery-based strategy, undergo development and change as the fieldwork progresses: some categories and category systems may be dropped, others may emerge as the research takes shape and sharpens its focus. In my own research on staffroom talk I began by collecting the exchanges I had recorded in my field-notes according to whether they related to the teachers' views of pupils on the one hand or to other aspects of teaching and the life of teachers on the other. As the analysis progressed I started searching through the data gathering together exchanges related to more refined and theoretically relevant categories, for example those concerned with the 'crisis' which the teachers saw facing them, those involving the trading of 'news' about pupils, those explaining why pupil performances were so 'bad' despite the teachers' best efforts, those relating to the ways in which the teachers sought to ease their task etc.

2.6   Having broken the data up into chunks suitable for analysis, the next step is to look at each piece of data and see what can be made of it. In doing this, however, there are methodological issues which must not be lost sight of, consideration of which may also throw up interesting ideas worthy of further development.

3   The Process of Analysis: Methodological Considerations

3.1   In ethnographic research the researcher himself is treated as part of the setting. The argument is, in part, that the presence and actions of the researcher may affect the phenomena under study and therefore must be documented in order to assess the effects of reactivity and to facilitate triangulation. But investigating the social interaction between researcher and those being studied may also provide useful data on participants, how they respond to particular kinds of outsider for example. You may remember that Berreman's (1962) analysis of his research was instructive in this respect.

3.2   One of the major considerations involved in the analysis of ethnographic data, therefore, is to determine the role of the circumstances of data collection in its production. In other words, whatever its form, it is not to be taken at face value, as unproblematically representing the world it is supposed to describe. Only by investigating the processes by which it was generated can we determine its implications and decide what inferences can legitimately be drawn from it. In the rest of this section I shall discuss some of the considerations that must be borne in mind while analysing data from different sources, considerations which are relevant to both the generation and the testing of theories.

Audience

3.3   One of the primary considerations in analysing data from almost any source is the audience to which the actions or accounts reported were directed. Whether the data represent what was said in an interview, actions which were observed or the content of documents, they will have been shaped to one degree or another by people's expectations regarding who might observe or hear about what they are saying or doing. Furthermore, some potential audiences, particularly those with crucial power resources, will be regarded as more important than others. Thus, for example, people producing documents write with certain kinds of audiences in mind, and for certain purposes. These considerations will shape the nature of the document through what is taken as relevant, what can be assumed to be existing knowledge, what should not be said, what must be said even if it is untrue etc. In my own investigation of staffroom talk I was very aware that different things could be said in different company. For example, a colleague would rarely, if ever, be criticized to his face: criticism of him behind his back, however, was quite commonplace. However, 'behind his back' meant not just when *he* was not there, but also when no one was there who would feel an obligation to report what was said to him. The point is that we must interpret differently what is said 'in public' and what is said 'in private' since to which category a statement belongs may have important consequences for how it relates to attitudes and actions in other contexts. However, whether something is 'in private' or 'in public' is not always obvious; one may have to know a setting very well in order to be able to recognize the public or private status of actions.

3.4   The role of the ethnographer himself must, of course, be taken into account as a potentially significant member of the audience. However, while an ethnographer's presence may have some effects on the situation being studied, the effect normally will be minimal, since the actors are operating under other, usually more important, considerations of interest and constraint besides those relating to the researcher. While there are circumstances and times when the ethnographer can find himself a central determinant of events in the situation he is studying, the whole character of ethnographic research practices is designed to avoid this. This is the point of going to 'natural' settings rather than relying on interview or laboratory situations; this is also one of the reasons why the ethnographer spends a lengthy period of time in the field, and spends much of that time seeking to develop trust among participants. Nevertheless, the data must be analysed with the possible effects of the ethnographer's presence and actions in mind.

3.5 Some of the methods ethnographers use involve greater danger of the researcher becoming the primary audience than others. This is true, for example, of documents solicited by the researcher himself; it is also true of interviews. In single rather than group interviews especially, the interviewee's conception of the researcher will affect what is said and what is not said and how it is said, via what he regards as relevant to the occasion as well as what he decides must be covered up or denied. His conception of the interviewer will derive in part, no doubt, from stereotypes of that role, but the knowledge he has built up about that ethnographer and his research over the course of the fieldwork will also be important. The ethnographer probably stands both to gain and lose from this (though the same argument can be made about the development of 'rapport' in non-ethnographic interviews). He will gain because he can trade on the trust and rapport he has built up in the field. He may lose though because the informant may believe he knows what the researcher is interested in and may not provide information which is actually of great relevance. This is especially likely if the ethnographer has not disclosed his purposes to participants or has disguised them. We have something of a dilemma here: the more informants take over the ethnographer's relevances in talking to him, the more useful they may be in one sense, as providers of information to which the ethnographer may not otherwise have access, but the less useful they may be as direct sources of data on participant perspectives.

3.6 Just as important as the knowledge the interviewee has built up about the ethnographer over the course of the fieldwork are the interpretations he makes about what the interviewer is interested in and asking for over the course of the interview itself. By his questions and responses, however 'neutral', the interviewer is providing the respondent with data by which he can reconstruct his conception of the interviewer's identity, interests and prejudices. Also important, and related, is the nature of the questions asked: do they naturally arise for the interviewee or do they require him to reflect on his experience, thereby reprocessing that experience into other categories to provide a response? If they are 'naturally' occurring questions are they highly charged with interests? One must recognize the possibility that what one is tapping may be highly developed and sophisticated rationales. For example, if one asks teenage lads why they engage in vandalism and they reply 'there's nothing else to do round here' or if we ask them why they belong to a gang and they reply that the gang provides protection against other gangs, how should we treat these answers? Do they genuinely reflect the reasons underlying gang membership or are they stock accounts used to justify gang membership to outsiders? I should warn you that the problem can arise with all categories of actor and that resolution of such issues is not easy.

3.7 In this connection Becker (1958) recommends that the ethnographer distinguish in his analysis between statements which are direct responses to his questions and those which are volunteered. This is certainly an important distinction to bear in mind, but we must remember that even 'spontaneous' utterances may be shaped to certain conceptions of the interviewer[1]. However, the interviewer may not be the only perceived audience. The informant may suspect that the interviewer will pass on or mention what he has said to others, or he may feel that he is speaking 'for posterity'. As with statements in 'natural' situations one must analyse interviews for the likely effects

---

[1]You may remember that Hargreaves and his colleagues (1975) found this in their attempt to avoid structuring teachers' discussions of deviant events in lessons (see Block 4, Part 3).

of the perceived audience on what is said. Actions and statements produced under different circumstances will have differing implications.

Surrounding Context

3.8   Whether the data concerned derive from participation, observation or documents we must take into consideration the background against which the actions or statements were produced. We must remember that what people say and do is sequentially related, that is, what they say and do is produced in the context of a developing sequence of interaction. Without interpreting accounts and actions in relation to these various backgrounds we may make quite incorrect inferences. One of the troubles is that our methodological practices inevitably cut us off from knowledge of some of these backgrounds unless we take precautions. This is another reason why staying in a setting for a relatively long period of time is advantageous. It also motivates the ethnographer's use of interviews and documents to complement his participant observation.

SAQ 2

If I ask a teacher what he finds to be the major problems in his work:

(a)   in what way might the 'surrounding context' affect his answer?

(b)   in what way might the 'perceived audience' influence his answer?

You should spend about fifteen minutes answering this question.

3.9   In the case of interviews the way in which the interview fits into the respondent's life must be investigated. The greater the degree of formality involved, the more remote may be the relationship between what is said in the interview and what is said and done in everyday life. On the other hand, with more informal interviews, in particular, the analyst must try to determine the degree to which the responses have been affected by recent experiences and how typical those experiences are. In this, as with all these considerations, it is not a matter of accepting or rejecting data, but rather of knowing *how* to interpret them; there is a great temptation to *assume* that actions, statements or interview responses represent stable features of the person or settings. With documents we must consider their whole mode of production: by whom they were initiated (documents are often requested or demanded by someone other than the author), what events stimulated them, and what processes they went through before they reached their final form. There are often several 'authors' of documents operating at different stages of their production, employing different relevances and operating under different kinds of constraint.

Social Location of the Actor, Informant or Author

3.10   People's social locations, that is, the patterns of social relationships in which they are enmeshed, can have two kinds of effects on the nature of the accounts or actions they produce. Firstly, social, physical and temporal locations determine the kind of information available to people. Such locations clearly affect what it is possible for people to see and hear 'at first hand'; they also determine what people will get to know about and how they will get to know things 'second hand'. The second way in which social location affects actions and accounts is through the particular perspectives which people in various social locations tend to generate and which will filter their understanding and knowledge of the world. In particular, the interpretation of information available to a person is likely to be selected and slanted in line with his prevailing interests and concerns. There may even be a strong element of wish-fulfilment involved.

3.11   In line with these two kinds of effect there are two major kinds of uses to which data can be put. The data can either be analysed for what they say about the world in which people live, using these people as informants, as apprentice researchers; alternatively, the data can be examined for what they say about the actors themselves, their perspectives on the world and the effects of their social location on those perspectives. Both kinds of analysis are important and should proceed simultaneously, and the impact of social location is important for both. Where an interviewee is treated as *informant* the quality of the information he provides must be assessed in relation to what his social location facilitates and blocks and also for the kind of bias which it is likely to induce. In *respondent* analysis the concern with social location relates rather to the possibility of generalizing the perspective detected in his responses to other actors in the same category, and also, of course, to explaining this perspective. Take the following example:

informant analysis

respondent analysis

> ((Extract from a discussion between teacher and researcher in school staffroom.))
> **T:**   The real trouble is the lower class group of people, yobos with empty heads. There's a terrible disease sweeping the population. The yobos will outbreed the sensible people because they won't use birth control while the sensible people will. Also since the yobos tend to get married earlier and have children earlier they have shorter generations, there's a very real danger that they'll outbreed thinking people.
> (Hammersley, field-notes)

Faced with this, if it is relevant to one's research problem, it is necessary to discover, somehow, whether this is a view shared by all or most of the other members of the school staff, or by a fraction of them, or whether it is idiosyncratic. Of course, one might well not be concerned with whether they agreed with this particular account of why things are bad and getting worse (shorter generations leading to outbreeding) so much as whether the other teachers also regard the situation as bad and getting worse, and formulate the problem in class terms.

Typicality across Time, Persons, Groups, Settings

3.12   This problem is particularly obvious with introspective data on participation. One of the crucial issues is the degree to which the ethnographer's experience simulates that of actors. There are always a number of different types of actor in any setting. Some identities are virtually mutually exclusive, teacher and pupil for example, while others overlap, for instance member of the school, pupil, gang-member, friend. The target role-identity must be clearly specified and the data analysed for the degree to which it represents that identity. The time-period for which this description of the experience of incumbents of a particular role is held to apply and the typicality of the ethnographer's experience as compared with that of other incumbents of the role also have to be investigated. Where the research is secret, one source of atypicality – fellow actors' knowledge that the person playing the role is also a researcher – is eliminated. However, as we saw in Block 4, this does not eliminate all the sources of reactivity. For example, the researcher's own knowledge that he is 'really' a researcher and that he is only a temporary incumbent of the role may affect his experiences in it. The typicality of introspective data must be assessed by employing other sources of data, for instance by using interviews to assess the degree to which there can be generalization to the experiences of other actors in particular categories and over time.

3.13   However, this requirement is not peculiar to the method of introspection: similar considerations apply to observational data where the analyst has to assess the degree to which the reports are representative of the site at other times, of other sites, actors and groups in similar categories etc. Where there has been random sampling along these dimensions such judgements are facilitated. Assessments of typicality are also necessary with interview data. In the case of respondent analysis the assessment may relate to whether the attitudes elicited operate beyond the boundaries of the interview and, if so, to what aspects of the actor's life they are directly relevant. Alternatively, the assessment may be concerned with how many actors in similar or different categories share the perspective. A further problem arises here: we must take care not to *assume* that because a respondent has indicated a belief in *X* he also believes in *Y* and *Z*, simply because people who generally believe in *X* usually believe in *Y* and *Z*. This kind of overreaching of the data seems to have been built into many attitude scales (Merton, 1940). While this tendency is not *built into* ethnographic analysis, it is still a danger which must be guarded against. A similar problem arises in relation to different contexts: we cannot assume that what people do in one context will be consistent with what they do in others. Thus, we cannot easily infer what they do in one context from what they do in another.

3.14   With informant analysis the concern with typicality is similar to that relating to observation data: can the information provided be generalized across sites and time? With all assessments of typicality, the great problem is to decide on the categories which are relevant: what are the units to be compared and along what dimensions? There are literally an infinite number of bases for assessing typicality. Too often it is assessed on the basis of what are *assumed* – often for no very good theoretical reasons – to be important bases.

Take the example of a document produced by a teacher. How would you set about assessing the typicality of the perspective you have detected in the teacher's comments?

3.15   The usual way of doing this, even in much ethnographic work, is via the standard face-sheet data categories: age, sex, social class background, amount of education etc. But how do we know that *these* categories are the most important or that they are even relevant? We need to have some theoretical grounds for this and we also need to be sure that our questions do in fact measure these theoretically defined concepts. It may be that the kind of school the teacher attended as a pupil and his informal position within it, or the nature of his experiences as a teacher in previous schools, or other things entirely, are the critical factors. There are an infinite number of possibilities and it is only on the basis of theory that we can assess typicality. Too often in social research the dimensions along which typicality is assessed are the products of convenience.

Change over the Course of Data Collection

3.16   With data from participation, observation and interviews the analyst must remember that change may have occurred over the course of the data collection process itself. For example, changes in the nature of the audience during a particular sequence of interaction, whether in an interview or in a 'natural' setting, may change the nature of the action or result in different things being said. What consequences such changes have will depend on the particular patterning of constraints and interests involved in the setting under study. Similarly, how others treat the ethnographer-as-participant and how he experiences the role himself may alter, resulting in changes in the nature of the data (see Berreman, 1962). Such change may be maturational in character, for example as familiarity or distrust grows, or it may be temporary or recurrent, caused, for example, by the secret researcher's recurrent fears that his cover has been blown.

3.17   Change, independent of the research process, may be a feature of the object being studied, or it may be related to the research process in some way. The second possibility is most likely in interviews. The interviewee's assessment of who the audience is and the interests and existing knowledge of that audience may change over the course of the interview thereby modifying his notion of what is relevant and what must be disguised, and thus affecting what is and is not said on various topics at different points in the interview. Given the possibility of change, a useful strategy is to begin by analysing each interview as a whole, trying to reconstruct the interviewee's conception of the interviewer and other elements of the audience and the ways in which these may have changed over the course of the interview.

Recording

3.18   However much the ethnographer seeks to make his data concrete and complete, they will inevitably be selective and inferential. The amount of selectivity and inference can, of course, vary: with some methods, notably introspection, these are likely to be relatively great because of limited opportunities to record events at the time at which they happen. In interviews and observation more concrete and complete recording may be possible, especially if tape, video or film recording can be used. Even then, though there will still have been selectivity and inference in the process of recording (when the recorder was switched on, where it was placed etc.) and in transcription. The more these processes of selectivity and inference can be made explicit and assessed the better idea we will have of what inferences can be legitimately drawn from the data produced.

3.19   *Summary*   The kinds of methodological considerations I have discussed in this section must form a central and systematic part of data analysis. In particular they provide a basis for triangulation across different data sources. However, sometimes they seem to be used in an *ad hoc* way to resolve discrepancies; this amounts to little more than the explaining away of data which do not fit the analyst's preferred explanation. Failure to take such considerations into account at all can result in the production of descriptions and explanations which bear little resemblance to the world to which they are supposed to relate. One of the crucial principles of analysis in ethnography is that the researcher himself be included within the research focus. The process by which the data were produced, and his role in it, must be analysed.

4   The Process of Analysis: Generating and Testing Theory

4.1   In examining segments of data, therefore, one must keep in mind the ways in which the data were produced and thus what are and are not legitimate inferences to be drawn. But, of course, the aim of the analysis is to develop and test a model of some aspect of the setting under study as it operates independently of the researcher's presence.

4.2 Analysis operates simultaneously on many different levels of abstraction. The most basic one is that embodied in the data records themselves, where the aim is to produce a relatively concrete narrative. Of course, the construction of narrative involves a complex process of interpretation requiring knowledge of participant culture and awareness of the possibility of being misled by fronts. However, the ultimate aim of ethnographic research is not simply to produce a narrative record of events in particular situations but rather to develop explanations of those events and others like them. Intentions and motives must be located in relation to the actor's actions and statements on other occasions, to perspectives also employed by other actors, and to the situations, routine and novel, which the actor faces. Beyond the narrative level, then, the search is for more abstract categories which explain the actions, intentions and motivations that occur on particular occasions.

4.3 In the early stages of the fieldwork, when the concern is with generating promising theoretical ideas, an ethnographer may pick segments for analysis haphazardly or concentrate on those which seem relevant to his *foreshadowed problems*.

foreshadowed problem

SAQ 3

Consider the following comment by a teacher made in the staffroom to other teachers, but in the presence of an ethnographer.

> **T:** Johnson ((pupil)) conned me. I thought he was a reasonable lad, not intelligent, but keen and helpful, but now Jack ((teacher)) tells me that he's got the longest crime-sheet in the school.
> (Hammersley, field notes)

Does this extract suggest to you any lines of analysis that could be followed up by examining further extracts from staffroom discussions, interviews with the teachers, observations of their classroom activities etc? I am asking simply for possible productive lines of analysis, not for analyses which you think are true. Develop as many analytic points as you can; it does not matter if some of them are mutually exclusive.

There is of course no correct answer to this question. You should spend fifteen minutes on this analysis. At the end of the Part you will find my own ideas.

4.4 Promising lines of analysis do not necessarily come easily and even when they do they must be developed, not left at the level of interesting possibilities. There are many different ways in which any object can be described and there are no logical procedures which we can use for finding theoretically productive categories and properties. There are, however, various strategies which can be used as aids to the sluggish imagination and for the systematic development of theoretical ideas. These strategies may be employed at any and indeed many stages in the research: they may play a role in pre-fieldwork research design, but equally can be usefully drawn on in post-fieldwork analysis as well as being used to direct the process of data collection itself.

Can you think of any ways in which one might try to generate analytic ideas?

4.5　One strategy involves the use of an existing theoretical model or analogy, the research taking the form of an attempt to develop and specify it by applying it to data from a particular setting. Ball's work (1972) on the abortion clinic which you read in association with Block 1 provides an example of this kind of approach. The concepts of 'self', 'identity', 'rhetoric' etc. had already been developed in a speculative way by social theorists.[2] A similar strategy is the application of a theory generated to deal with one kind of social phenomenon to another area. Thus for example, Hargreaves, Hester and Mellor (1975) applied labelling theory[3], which had been developed by sociologists in the area of crime and social deviance, to deviance in classrooms. Such models and analogies can provide an important starting-point for analysis but what is involved here is not a matter of simply testing or applying existing theory to a new area or setting; it is expected that the theory will be developed and perhaps transformed in the process.

4.6　Another kind of lever is the 'filling in' of missing elements in the existing literature or in an existing theory. An example is the work of Hargreaves (1967) and Lacey (1970) on streaming and the formation of subcultures in schools. One of the guiding ideas of both authors seems to have been the 'filling in' of Albert Cohen's (1955) theory of delinquent subculture formation. Cohen had argued that male delinquency is largely working class, that it is by nature negativistic, malicious and non-utilitarian, and that these features represent the inverse of middle class values. He argues that working class boys tend to adopt these values as a result of their frustration in being unable to achieve valued identities in terms of middle class values. This 'failure' derives from the fact that working class culture does not provide the necessary cognitive resources and attitudes to facilitate 'success'. He suggests, moreover, that school is the crucial arena where this failure and frustration occur, though he does not investigate school processes.[4] Hargreaves and Lacey sought to document this inversion of values and to investigate those aspects of school which produced it. However, once again the theory was modified in the process.

4.7　The ethnographer's stress on 'process' is a general response of this kind to mainstream sociology's neglect of the ways in which social phenomena are generated. In Block 3 Paul Atkinson pointed to the recent trend in the sociology of education towards the investigation of social interaction in schools. Sally Macintyre (1977) provides an example of this orientation in a different field:

> Approximately one-fifth of all conceptions, and an even higher proportion of first conceptions, in Britain in the early 1970s were to single women. There are four common outcomes of pregnancy for single women: marriage to the putative father; induced abortion; remaining single and keeping the baby; and remaining single and giving the baby up for adoption. It is known that

[2]*Notably by George Herbert Mead, an American philosopher whose work has been developed by the symbolic interactionist school of sociology. See, for example, Blumer (1969) and Goffman (1968a).*

[3]*For accounts of labelling theory, see paragraph 1.4 of this Part and Becker (1963).*

[4]*See Downes (1966) or Taylor, Walton and Young (1973) for more detailed accounts of Cohen's theory and its competitors.*

the incidence of these outcomes has changed from time to time, as have, of course, the relevant social attitudes, social policy and legislation, and these have been the subject of demographic and historical studies. Yet little is known about how these outcomes are reached, or how these may be affected by social attitudes, policies and legislation.

This book aims to complement existing extensive and social structural studies with an intensive, detailed study of the pregnancy careers of some

Figure 1   The pregnancy careers of the women interviewed in the gynaecological ward and mother and baby home

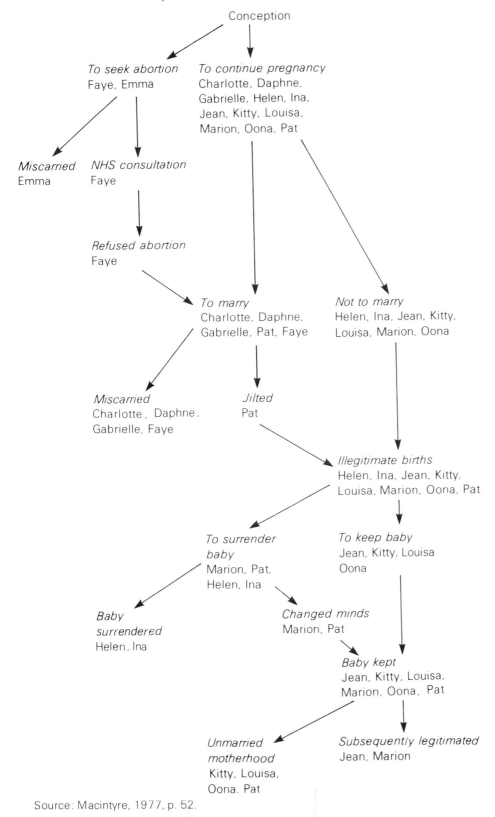

Source: Macintyre, 1977, p. 52.

single women in a Scottish City between 1971 and 1974. The study was designed to examine the processes by which these women reached a particular outcome of pregnancy: what their pregnancy meant to them and to others, what happened when they came into contact with doctors and social workers, and how decisions on this matter are made. (Macintyre, 1977, p. 9)

Some sense of the complexities involved in the process of reaching these four outcomes can be gauged from Figure 1. A more routine kind of 'filling in' may also occur where an area of parallel importance to that on which attention has hitherto been focused is investigated. For example, while many have investigated teachers' categorizations of pupils and their consequences, only fairly recently have pupils' typifications of teachers become a focus of inquiry (see Furlong, 1977).

4.8 Sometimes unstructured interviews are used to generate theoretical categories. Participants' accounts of their life and world are elicited and the analysis is focused on themes which emerge from those accounts, for example, routine troubles, crises, factional differences etc. Such themes provide a set of issues around which to start to structure analysis and perhaps collect further data. Peter Woods' (1976) research on the importance to pupils of 'having a laugh' provides an example. Using open-ended interviews to explore pupils' experience of school, Woods found that 'having a laugh' was a recurrent theme and thus set about classifying types of laughter and their functions.

4.9 Fictionalized, semi-fictionalized and autobiographical literature can in a similar way provide the analyst with very useful starting ideas. Many sources which for the purposes of *testing* theory have very limited usefulness, unless one's research is particularly concerned with the ways in which such documents are produced, can be a very useful aid in generating theory. Indeed the most unlikely sources can prove valuable. Women's magazines provide an illuminating example: they can provide ideas on all manner of topics from images of the woman's role, through aspects of the lives of pop stars, to the effects on personal life of various kinds of crises. Newspaper articles are a similar source.

see Block 2, Part 2b

SAQ 4
Consider the following letter to a national newspaper. Does it suggest any interesting ideas to you, for example relationships between social mobility, class and people's images of society?

Trendies versus Strivers

Sir,—Jill Tweedie in her article on the William Tyndale school (October 27) is right — almost.

She is most certainly right in her analysis of class-based parent behaviour. And she is most definitely and triumphantly right in pin-pointing the essentially anti-democratic, elitist attitude of the teaching staff. The whole idea of 'educating for the year 2000' is fundamentally obnoxious to the true democrat as Plato's Guardians or the Hitler Youth, when it is pursued without the consent of the majority.

Where she is not quite correct is in polarising the issue purely on a class basis. It would seem to me, as a new bourgeois technocrat from a proletarian family, that the real dichotomy is between the 'strivers' and the 'trendies'.

The strivers are those who know through upbringing or experience that the world is a hard tough place, and there is a profound psychological satisfaction to be had from succeeding. They know that success requires hard graft and are consequently achievment oriented.

The trendies (I call them that because they are, regrettably, in the mainstream of fashionable English 'progressive' opinion) have woolly romantic notions about the quality of life and believe it is more important to be happy than successful. They are bolstered in their beliefs by the evidence around them of a welfare state, government subsidies, and the general erosion of the concept of personal responsibility.

The saddest part of the story is that the trendies will end by doing their children a positive harm. It is clear that as our economic situation degenerates and our fragile social welfare structure starts to fray at the edges it will be the 'strivers' who succeed (or at the worst survive).

I hope that the trendies will be as happy in successful penury as they would be in unsuccessful affluence.

B. D. Green.

Kingston Upon Thames,
Surrey.

Source: The Guardian

4.10 Once ideas have started to emerge the analysis must become rather more systematic. One technique frequently used at this stage of the research is *theoretical sampling* (see Block 3, Part 5, paragraphs 2.7 to 2.9).

theoretical sampling

Outline the process of theoretical sampling.

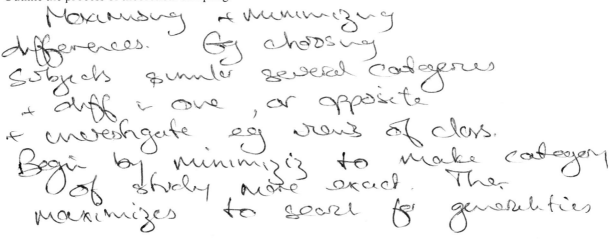

4.11 What is involved here is multiple comparisons of different groups and settings, each comparison or round of comparisons being selected so as to further the development of the emerging theory. What groups or settings are to be sampled is not decided before the fieldwork begins, as is usually the case in survey research, but recurrently as the fieldwork continues. The researcher usually begins by minimizing the differences between comparison groups so as to bring out the basic properties of a category. Subsequently however, he begins to make comparisons which maximize differences so as to discover the more universal uniformities.

4.12 When samples of data have been drawn from different groups or settings, the researcher analyses segments of data, using ideas which emerged in the previous stage of the analysis, but also developing further categories. Each segment is taken in turn and, its relevance to one or more categories having been noted, it is compared with other segments of data similarly categorized, with a view to developing typologies within the category, relating that category to others etc.

> The analyst starts thinking in terms of the full range of types or continua of the category, its dimensions, the conditions under which it is pronounced or minimized, its major consequences, its relation to other categories, and its

other properties. For example, while constantly comparing incidents on how nurses respond to the social loss of dying patients, we realized that some patients are perceived as a high social loss and others as a low social loss, and that patient care tends to vary positively with degree of social loss. It was also apparent that some social attributes that nurses combine to establish a degree of social loss are seen immediately (age, ethnic group, social class), while some are learned after time is spent with the patient (occupational worth, marital status, education). This observation led us to the realization that perceived social loss can change as new attributes of the patients are learned. It also became apparent, from studying the comparison groups, under what conditions (types of wards and hospitals) we would find clusters of patients with different degrees of social loss. (Glaser and Strauss, 1968, p. 106)

As this process continues the emerging model will become more and more developed, with categories being related to one another in various ways and their internal structure more clearly displayed.

> ... The diverse properties ... start to become integrated. Thus, we soon found that the calculating and recalculating of social loss by nurses was related to their development of a social loss 'story' about the patient. When asked about a dying patient, nurses would tell what amounted to a story about him. The ingredients of this story consisted of a continual balancing out of social loss factors as the nurses learned more about the patient. Both the calculus of social loss and the social loss story were related to the nurse's strategies for coping with the upsetting impact on her professional composure of, say, a dying patient with a high social loss (e.g. a mother with two children). This example further shows that the category becomes integrated with other categories of analysis: the social loss of the dying patient is related to how nurses maintain professional composure while attending his dying. Thus the theory develops, as different categories and their properties tend to become integrated through constant comparisons that force the analyst to make some related theoretical sense of each comparison. (Glaser and Strauss, 1968, p. 107)

4.13   Theoretical sampling and the use of this *constant comparative method* are ways in which emergent ideas can be developed into a model of social processes occurring in the setting. However, they do not provide a rigorous and systematic test of the model. For this the ethnographer must rely on *analytic induction*, a form of the comparative method in which there is a systematic search for falsifying evidence and modification of the theory until no further disconfirming evidence can be found. This strategy may be employed both within the study of a particular setting to check the validity of descriptions and explanations of processes there, or on a larger scale to try to establish universal patterns of causality across all relevant groups and settings, as in the work of Lindesmith (1947) on opiate addiction and Cressey (1950) on embezzlement.

constant comparative method

analytic induction

SAQ 5

Read the article by Donald R. Cressey, 'The criminal violation of financial trust'. This reports one of the classic examples of the use of analytic induction to establish a universal causal explanation. While reading it you should try to identify any implications the sampling strategy and data sources employed by Cressey may have for his claim to have established a universal causal explanation.

Now read Cressey (1950)

4.14   You may perhaps recognize some similarity between analytic induction and Popper's emphasis on the importance of attempts to falsify hypotheses

(Block 1, Part 3, section 7). Thus both Cressey (1950) and Lindesmith (1947) were concerned to develop theories which were universally applicable and they explicitly searched for negative cases; though, as I have said, Cressey does not actually set out to find cases which are most likely to falsify his theory.

SAQ 6

Consider the article by Ball (1972) on the abortion clinic which you read for Block 1. In that article the author leaves his analysis at the level of the application and development of a set of ideas about self, identity etc.
What steps might you take:

(a)   to develop the theory further?

(b)   to test it?

This question should take about fifteen minutes.

4.15   The concern with producing a theory which is universally applicable is relatively rare in the ethnographic tradition. Indeed many ethnographers would suggest that it is impossible to find universal laws of human behaviour, one piece of evidence being that few, if any, such laws have been satisfactorily corroborated despite the massive expansion of social science in this century. However, whatever may be the truth of that, analytic induction can be, and has been, effectively used to test accounts of social processes *within* particular cultures, and *within* particular settings.

4.16   There is considerable variation in the nature of the products of ethnographic research projects. They can range from what are little more than narrative accounts of events in a setting, through the development of typologies, to more complex, perhaps causal, models. Krain (1974) provides a fairly typical example of the typology, outlining four strategies by which enlisted men in the US Army Reserve sought to avoid week-end Task Assignments.

> 1   *The Prior Assignment*   The enlisted man claims he already has a task, making it impossible to start a new one.
>
> 2   *Urgent Situation*   A long-standing foul-up, examples of which are plentiful in the Army, is related to the superior as an urgent situation that must be attended to now.
>
> 3   *Incapacity*   The assignment cannot be accepted for reasons of sickness (a relatively rare excuse), permanent medical restrictions, lack of technical knowledge, or lack of legal right (as in driving a vehicle or operating a projector).
>
> 4   *Shunning*   The assignment is laughed off as 'not serious' and the decliner withdraws. 'The aim . . . may be to convince the NCO that the EM is really too nice a guy (because he is "funny" and "hip") to be assigned such a task. It may also be a kind of smokescreen. The enlisted man confuses the superior by the use of humor and withdraws in a cloud of guffaws from the superior's visual field with the final responsibility for completing the task not firmly placed.'
> (Krain, 1974, quoted in Lofland, 1976, pp. 112–13)

4.17   Such typologies provide a basis for the development of theoretical models. Thus Cressey (1950) links together typologies relating to kinds of financial problem, strategies for solving them and rationalizations to produce a model of the process by which someone comes to commit trust violation:

(a)   A person acquires a financial problem which he dare not reveal to others.

(b)   He realizes that the problem can be secretly resolved by violation of a position of financial trust.

(c)   He must be able to rationalize or normalize his deviance to himself, for example on the grounds that he is just borrowing the money to tide him over and will be able to pay it back later.

But the development of such a model, and even more so the testing of it, may be a collaborative product of several different studies in different settings.

4.18   The products of ethnographic work also vary in level of abstraction.

Outline the distinction made in Block 3, Part 5 between topical and generic problems.

Block 3, Part 5, para. 2.5

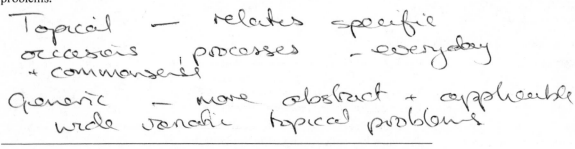

Topical — relates specific occasions, processes — everyday + commonsense

Generic — more abstract + applicable wide variety topical problems

---

4.19   Mirroring the distinction between topical and generic problems, some ethnographers have distinguished between substantive and formal theory (for example, see Glaser and Strauss, 1968). *Substantive theory* is concerned with relatively concrete areas like race relations, mentally handicapped children, blackmail etc. At a higher level of abstraction *formal theories* can be developed which describe and explain processes which occur in very different substantive areas. Thus the substantive areas mentioned above are all relevant to the formal theory of stigma, that is, the disqualification of a person from full social acceptance (Goffman, 1968b). Substantive and formal theories are not qualitatively different forms of theory but represent two sections of a continuum of abstraction. Once again substantive and formal theories are equally valued and the development of formal theory is often a collaborative product rather than being achieved from scratch within a single research project.

substantive theory

formal theory

4.20   *Summary*   In the last three sections, I have outlined the considerations and procedures involved in the analysis of ethnographic data for the generation, development and testing of theory. It must be remembered, however, that there is considerable diversity among ethnographers in the procedure used; this account probably represents the mainstream approach to ethnographic data analysis.

5   Writing Up and Publishing the Research Report

5.1   Research reports in the other two traditions are generally written to a fairly standard pattern: the hypotheses to be tested are stated first, the research procedures outlined, the findings analysed, and finally an interpretation of the findings is given. The diverse and discovery-based character of ethnographic research makes any such standard pattern of reporting impossible. In any case, ethnographers, in line with their suspicion of fronts, often feel that this standard pattern of reporting employed by the other styles disguises as much as it reveals. The form which ethnographic reports take is thus largely a product of the particular course the research has followed, the report usually being structured around certain major themes which emerged as the fieldwork and analysis progressed. However, there are certain general principles which underly the construction of ethnographic research reports.

On the basis of your reading of Block 4, Part 3 you ought to be able to say what one of these is.

5.2 Perhaps the most distinctive feature of ethnographic analysis is the emphasis on reflexivity: description and analysis of the research process itself. One important element of reflexivity in connexion with research reporting is the provision of extracts from the data. This provides a basis for the reader's assessment of the study: it gives him some idea of how the ethnographer interpreted his data as well as some materials with which he can attempt various kinds of re-analysis. Some selection is inevitable in the presentation of data to the reader; the whole running record cannot be published. Often quotations from the data records seem to be chosen simply to illustrate the argument. That is certainly an important function but it should not be the only one. Illustrations ought to be given from each stage of the analysis, and the set of illustrations provided for each stage needs to be representative of the body of data used. Of particular interest and importance are deviant cases, these should be presented to the reader even if the analyst has found no way of incorporating them into his analysis. The fact that there are such cases does not necessarily undermine the theory, nor does it mean they cannot be incorporated into it, others may find ways of doing this. Unfortunately, you will find that despite the attention paid by ethnographers to the process of research many accounts of research findings are still insufficiently systematic and reflexive in this respect.

5.3 Thus, for example, many studies of school processes employ case studies of particular pupils to illustrate and support their arguments. However, the basis for their selection often remains obscure. Lacey provides a notable exception:

> The case studies . . . have been selected to illustrate the nature of the relationship between a number of the major social factors relevant to this book – academic achievement, social class and parental encouragement. The cases have been selected with the aid of the paradigm below to cover the full range of possible combinations of these factors.

Parental interest and encouragement	Middle class		Working class	
	High achiever	Low achiever	High achiever	Low achiever
High	A Martin	B Baker	C Welenski	D Buttle
Low	E French	F Russell	G King	H Howells, Docker

Source: Lacey, 1970, p. 125

5.4   The situation is similar with the other aspect of reflexivity: the provision of an account of how the research was done, a natural history. You read what is perhaps still the best example of this genre for Block 3 – William Foote Whyte's (1955) account of his research on an Italian-American 'slum'. While most ethnographers find it necessary to provide some kind of account of their research for the reader, these are often of a fairly superficial and selective character.

Furthermore, they often seem to have a dash of rhetorical self-justification about them. You must bear this possibility in mind whenever you read such accounts.[5]

5.5   The way in which research is written up for publication is not governed only by methodological criteria, of course; political and ethical considerations are also relevant.

At this point you should read the article by Howard S. Becker, 'Problems in the publication of field studies', which you will find in the Principles and Procedures Reader (Ch. 24). As Becker makes clear, the more one succeeds in penetrating official fronts and self-deceptions, the greater the chance of conflict with some section of the participants over the publication of the findings.

Now read Becker (1964)

5.6   We have to ask, then, where the ethnographer's responsibilities lie. There are a number of different views on this. Some argue that participants must be the ultimate arbiters. Davies and Kelly (1976) seem to come close to this position, though clearly they were also under pressure to adopt this position given the response of the 'clients'.[6] Those adopting this view often regard it as necessary to get the specific permission of all participants for any kind of publication: the tapes and field-notes which the researcher has collected are regarded as belonging to the participants. Often such researchers are engaged in action research and regard their political role as one of broker, mediating the views of the different groups in the situation so as to maximize mutual understanding. Others also see their role as an explicitly political one, but this time they adopt an adversary orientation towards participants. They argue that much previous social research has been of the powerless for the powerful and they set out to reverse this, their research targets being elites and bureaucracies.[7] Their aim is to make such organizations publicly, democratically accountable. Given this goal their ethical responsibilities are, as they see it, to the 'public' or 'the people' and almost any research strategy, no holds barred, is legitimate.

5.7   The third position I want to outline, and the one I would advocate, was, and perhaps still is in many quarters, the conventional wisdom. This view underlies the article by Becker and is summed up in his phrase 'the ethic of scientific inquiry'. In these terms the researcher is *bound primarily* to the requirements of science as an enterprise justifiable in itself, as ultimately being of potential benefit to all,

---

[5]There are some useful collections of research biographies: see, for example, Bell and Newby (1977), Vidich, Bensman and Stein (1964), Bowen (1954), Douglas (1972), Freilich (1970), Habenstein (1970), Hammond (1964), Powdermaker (1966), Shipman (1976), Spindler (1970) and Wax (1971).

[6]But see my discussion of SAQ 4 in Block 4, Part 3.

[7]The work of Spencer (1973) on West Point (see Block 4, Part 3, paragraph 3.3) falls into this category.

increasing our understanding of ourselves and our world. The ethic of science requires analysis and publication to be constrained as little as possible by political or ethical considerations. While the social sciences cannot ignore the consequences of their work, they are not *wholly* responsible for them, nor should specific political objectives be their goal. To the degree that they do take on specific objectives there tends to be an insistence that only those questions be asked which have the most apparent and immediate relevance to particular political positions and the biasing effects of political values on the production of knowledge tend to be enhanced. This is not to deny that there may still be times when publication must be avoided or delayed because of its consequences either for political goals or for participants. And at all times, as far as possible, participants must be protected from any consequences of the research by the maintenance of anonymity in the research report.

5.8 However, there are times when anonymity may be very difficult to achieve. For example, Vidich and Bensman (1958) found it impossible to conceal successfully the identities of those occupying leading positions in Springdale.[8] In such situations there are no hard and fast rules, the researcher must evaluate for himself the considerations on each side. However, the ethic of science must be a primary consideration in such deliberations.

6 Conclusions

6.1 In this Part of the course I have tried to give you some idea of the ways in which ethnographers analyse their material and some of the considerations which go into the writing and publication of ethnographic research reports. As I remarked earlier, ethnographers have generally been less concerned with quantification and statistical analysis and more concerned with the problems involved in interpreting actions correctly and with building their theory from the social meanings embedded in those actions. The nature of ethnographic analysis largely derives from that orientation.

Activity 1
In conclusion I suggest you read the article by David Sudnow entitled 'Normal crimes: sociological features of the penal code in a Public Defender Office'. This is a well-known and highly regarded ethnographic account, but this is not to say you must read it uncritically. As you read it you should consider any methodological considerations arising from his use of data, the theoretical levels which Sudnow seems to have used, the nature of the product of his analysis, and the validity of his interpretations. In other words you should assess the ways in which it is satisfactory and those in which it is less satisfactory as a piece of ethnographic research and consider how the account it presents could be developed and tested further.

Now read Sudnow (1965)

Spend an hour reading the article and half an hour evaluating it. You will find my comments with the answers to the Self-assessment Questions.

---

[8] *The Springdale controversy was referred to in the Becker article (1964; set reading).*

Objectives

After working through this Part you should be able to:

1 Explain why ethnographers do not make the production of statistically manipulable data their primary concern (paragraph 1.1).

2 Distinguish between explanation by covering-law and explanation-by-understanding and outline the rationale underlying the latter (paragraphs 1.3 to 1.10).

3 Outline the process by which ethnographic data are analysed (section 2).

4 Demonstrate an understanding of the various methodological considerations involved in ethnographic data analysis (section 3).

5 Outline some of the strategies that can be used to generate promising lines of analysis (paragraphs 4.1 to 4.9).

6 Demonstrate the nature and role of theoretical sampling and analytic induction (paragraphs 4.10 to 4.20).

7 Explain the importance and form of reflexivity as it relates to the research report (pargraphs 5.2 to 5.4).

8 Spell out the various considerations and pressures involved in the publication of field studies (paragraphs 5.5 to 5.7).

Answers to Self-assessment Questions and Activities

Please note that, as with the questions and activities in previous Parts dealing with ethnography (Block 3, Part 5 and Block 4, Part 3), some of these 'answers' require personal judgement and opinion; what follows are my judgements. They do not constitute the only possible answers to the questions.

SAQ 1

There are, of course, many different strategies that could be adopted. For example, one might use interviews or 'natural talk' in some setting to investigate the concepts relevant to social status which people use in everyday life, and how to use them. Alternatively, one might look at particular settings which are likely to have significance for social status considerations. For example, one could examine teachers' categorizations of their pupils to see whether they were informed by a concern with the social status of their families and, if so, the conception of status and its distribution underlying these (see Becker, 1970a). Then again, with the same kind of interest, one might investigate marriage agencies or any kind of voluntary association or organization that also functions as a marriage market, for example churches and universities. Yet another possibility is that people display social status by the way they dress (Stone, 1970), though we would have to take account of the fact that people also select and arrange their dress according to setting. However, that might provide a new insight for us since I suspect that not just people but also settings are assigned differential status.

Of course, with all these strategies there is a problem of generalization – can the findings be generalized to other members of the society, to other settings, to other times etc.? This can be assessed by further research; one does at least have an account of how social status works in one 'natural' setting. The survey approach, on the other hand, runs the risk of producing findings which bear only the remotest relation to what normally occurs in the society, without the intervention of the social scientist.

SAQ 2

(a)   It is worth considering exactly what this question is asking for. The teacher is being asked to analyse his experience and decide which are the most recurrent and serious problems that face him. One possibility is that a problem which had recently 'come to a head' might gain prominence simply because of its recent character; people do not seem to view their past experience with an indifference to time: things which were experienced as make-or-break crises may, months or years later, take on the character of jokes and vice versa. This occurs partly because events take on different kinds of significance as they fit into different patterns of subsequent events and partly because people's patterns of emotional investment change over time. One possibility which needs testing out is that answers to such a question may vary much less over time in the case of people who have been in the same situation for a long period of time and where a routine pattern of activity has arisen. The fact that the answers a person gives to this could vary considerably even over relatively short periods of time, should not, however, be seen as just a problem. It suggests something about people's experience which must be explored. Where it does endanger the validity of our interpretations it can perhaps be dealt with by repeat interviewing, or by the elicitation of life-history documents.

(b)   In answer to the second part of the question we need to consider what it might mean, what it might cost someone, to admit that they have problems. Teachers, like policemen, are in a curious bind here. On the one hand, to say that ignorance and ill-discipline (or crime) are rife is to lay the groundwork for receiving further resources and to make clear the importance and success-in-the-face-of-great-difficulty of teachers. On the other hand, it may be used to suggest that teachers in general are, or that this teacher in particular is, incompetent. We must analyse the response, then, with those kind of considerations in mind.

There is another kind of audience consideration that also arises. If we speculate that there are 'respectable' and 'unrespectable' points of view in societies and that proposing an 'unrespectable' point of view may call down disfavour upon oneself even from those who privately agree, how the teacher assesses the interviewer and whom he expects might also hear what he says can affect *what* he says. Thus, a teacher I once interviewed, in reply to this question, began by indicating that what he was about to say was 'off the record' he went on to comment that a particular ethnic minority was the biggest problem. In different circumstances I might not have received that reply.

SAQ 3

The following are the possible lines of analysis that struck me. I am sure that there are others.

'Reasonable lad, not intelligent, but keen and helpful' seems to be treated as incompatible with 'the longest crime-sheet in the school' so that knowledge of the latter forces reinterpretation of the behaviour which formed the basis for the former evaluation (in some sense 'having a long crime-sheet' is definitive, more reliable apparently than personal impressions). It may be that 'the longest crime-sheet in the school' is being used as short-hand for a lot of other things Jack said and that for some reason Jack is seen as being likely to know this pupil best, for instance maybe he is his form-master.

The fact that the pupil has a long 'crime-sheet' even though he appeared 'reasonable' can be taken by the teachers to show just how slippery and deceitful these pupils can be. 'Delinquent activities' outside are obviously taken to have implications for what pupils might do or for what they must in fact have been doing all along in school.

Any activity requires some categorization of the phenomena to be dealt with, on the basis of their relevant typical features. The teachers work in classrooms under important constraints of time, vision and number of simultaneous concerns. They are always 'on stage' in the classroom; they claim authority to control what goes on in there and therefore anything 'untoward' which happens potentially damages their authority, and may possibly encourage further deviation by pupils from the rules of 'proper' classroom behaviour. An aid in the problem of control adopted by teachers as by others with similar problems is to 'know what to expect' from different quarters. This minimizes, saying nothing of accuracy, the cues required to guess what's going on, who is involved, and in what roles. Knowing what 'type' a pupil is, is important otherwise one might be 'caught out'. Given the important but problematic nature of the interpretation of pupils' actions it is reasonable to expect the teachers to supplement their own observations with information from colleagues and it would seem that some talk in the staffroom has this function.

SAQ 4

This letter suggests a number of interesting possibilities to me. Firstly, it raises the question of whether conceptions of society, and more broadly social ideologies, are class-based. It suggests that the relationship between class position and ideological commitment may be rather complex. It also suggests that social mobility might have important consequences for a person's conception of society. Are there important differences in ideological viewpoint between people who have experienced rapid upward social mobility themselves and their children who are born at that 'higher' level and take it for granted? However, we would also, of course, want to clarify what we mean by 'social class' and 'social mobility'.

Another interesting point is that the distinction between two ideologies which the writer makes appears to be very similar to that which can be found among teachers, between 'progressives' and 'traditionals' and among probation officers, social workers, lawyers and other occupations. An example from the area of law is the competition between punishment and treatment ideals. The apparent ubiquity of this kind of split might prompt one to ask whether it is related to some very deep changes in the structure of industrial societies, for example from an emphasis on thrift, discipline, personal responsibility, the free market etc., to consumption, freedom, permissiveness, treatment, welfare etc. However, before investigating such a question we would need to investigate how accurately this dichotomy of views represented the situation within these various occupations and others and to what degree the first set of ideals has ever been the dominant one.

SAQ 5

From a sampling point of view one should note that Cressey investigated trust violaters who had been caught and imprisoned, and only those in a particular prison at a particular point in time. Furthermore, you should note the differential reliance on different informants. As regards data sources note that he relies on interviews. We can imagine that asking informants to recall their experience and reasons for action at some earlier point in time raises problems. This is especially the case when the focus is a set of events which may have been the topic of public, by no means neutral, and certainly consequential discussion in court as well as of subsequent private reflection.

While Cressey supplements his data by examining cases in the literature and cases collected by Sutherland (1949) earlier, we should note that he does not seem to search for negative cases by looking for situations in which his model seems most unlikely to hold. Nor does he go outside American society and thus he is not able to discount the possibility of cultural variation. These limitations reflect the difficulties of studying this topic but they must be borne in mind when interpreting his account.

SAQ 6

On the basis of Ball's article (1972) and other work on deviance we might think it useful to construct a typology of deviant interactions according to whether participants are habitual or occasional deviants (see the diagram below).

		Party A	
		Habitual	Occasional
Party B	Habitual	1	2
	Occasional	2	3

Investigations of these three situations would probably lead to the development of the theory and it would also provide something of a test. Thus, for example, we could investigate transactions between thieves and fences as a situation where both participants are 'habitual deviants'. Alternatively, we could draw on Humphreys's account of 'tearoom trade' (1970) though in some cases this might fit 3 better than 1. It might also be profitable to investigate other situations under the second category besides that of abortion. Prostitution might provide a useful example. Examples falling under the third category are more difficult to find, though they might be very illuminating. One possible source would be the beginnings of any kind of deviant group, for example where a gang of youths first begins to 'try out' vandalism (Cohen, 1955).

The most rigorous *test* of the theory would perhaps be the investigation of abortion clinics in places where abortion was not a criminal offence, and where, therefore, at least in legal terms, neither participant is deviant, even though the same activity is involved. If we were to find few differences between this legal abortion clinic and Ball's account then we may begin to doubt the relevance of the habitual-occasional deviant distinction to the explanation of those aspects of social process in abortion clinics with which Ball was concerned (though of course we might find other interesting differences which may send us off in another direction). We might, on the other hand, suspect that, even when legal, abortion may still be regarded as a morally disreputable activity and that therefore the participants are still deviant in a broader sense. In order to test this we could try to find some culture in which abortion was not even morally disreputable and investigate the social action surrounding abortion there.

A couple of things are important to note about this testing process, however. Firstly, it does not produce certainty; no testing strategy does that. Even if it turns out that the features described by Ball are present in the practice of abortion in the culture where it is not a morally disreputable activity, this may result from other differences between this culture and the society in which the original studies were done rather than being anything to do with the theory we are seeking to test. The second point follows on from this. The testing and development of theories are closely related to one another, they are not two entirely separate enterprises operating on different principles. In general, falsification of a hypothesis leads to a reconstruction of the theory, though there are, of course, occasions where it may be taken to justify the abandonment of a whole line of investigation, perhaps on the grounds that 'the wrong question' has been asked. Ethnographers are concerned to develop their theories to increase their scope and detail as well as to test them. The kind of strategies I have suggested here would do both to varying degrees.

Activity 1

Sudnow presents an account of the routine work of a particular Public Defender Office in the USA. He seems to imply that the findings can be generalized to all P.D. Offices but he specifically rules out generalization to all legal process, including some handled by P.D. Offices (what he calls 'special cases'). However, the extent to which the findings can be generalized to other P.D. Offices cannot be assessed from the account provided.

This article is fairly typical of ethnographic reports in its provision of reflexive information. There is some; thus, for example, on p. 248 he gives us some of the data he interpreted as indicating that the P.D. is part of the court unlike the Private Attorney. He also provides us with transcripts of first contacts. In other places, though (for example pp. 245–6 and the section at the bottom of p. 249), he gives us little idea of how he came to his conclusions. In particular, we do not know what role he played in eliciting and recording the data and how far the statements which he quotes representing the views of one P.D. can be generalized to all the others in the office – we need to know how he checked that they could be so generalized (see, for example, pp. 253–4). In fact we are not actually told how many P.D.s there are in the office.

There are clues in the article as to some of the analytic levers Sudnow has used to generate his account. The first few pages seem to indicate that his central orientation throughout was to apply an existing theoretical view about the sociological significance of legal categories. Another lever he seems to have employed is the comparison of the attitudes of P.D.s regarding the guilt of the defendant with those of Private Attorneys. This proves a very useful strategy indeed, pointing to the significance of the routine character of the P.D.'s work and of the way he operates as a court functionary.

Whether Sudnow engaged in any systematic analytic induction within the setting he was investigating in order to check out his theory is unclear, though he does mention and seek to account for special/deviant cases.

It seems to me, then, that we must treat this article as a very important first stage in the development of a theory of routine justice in the USA and of the role of the P.D. in that. There is still much development and testing of the theory required and we might hope that ethnographers begin to take their ideal of reflexivity much more seriously. I should point out that Sudnow's article is probably a better than average ethnographic account and that, sad to say, the same criticisms can be made of my own articles!

References

BALL, D. W. (1972) 'Self and identity in the context of deviance: the case of criminal abortion', in Scott, R. A. and Douglas, J. D. (eds) (1972) *Theoretical perspectives on deviance*, New York, Basic Books. Reprinted in Wilson, M. J. (ed.) (1979), Ch. 9.

BECKER, H. S. (1958) 'Problems of inference and proof in participant observation', *American Sociological Review*, Vol. 23, December, pp. 652–60. Reprinted in Becker, H. S. (1970b) and in Bynner, J. and Stribley, K. M. (eds) (1979), Ch. 23.

BECKER, H. S. (1963) *Outsiders*, New York, Free Press.

BECKER, H. S. (1964) 'Problems in the publication of field studies', in Vidich, A. J., Bensman, J. and Stein, M. R. (eds) (1964), pp. 267–84. Reprinted in Bynner, J. and Stribley, K. M. (eds) (1979), Ch. 24. (Set Reading.)

BECKER, H. S. (1970a) 'Social class variations in the teacher-pupil relationship', in Becker, H. S. (ed.) (1970b).

BECKER, H. S. (1970b) *Sociological work*, Harmondsworth, Allen Lane, The Penguin Press.

BELL, C. and NEWBY, H. (ed.) (1977) *Doing sociological research*, London, Allen and Unwin.

BERREMAN, G. D. (1962) 'Behind many masks: ethnography and impression management in a Himalayan village', Monograph No. 4, Society for Applied Anthropology, Ithaca, N.Y., Cornell University. (Supplied as Supplementary Material for Blocks 1–4.)

BLUMER, H. (1969) *Symbolic interactionism*, London, Prentice-Hall.

BOWEN, E. S. (1954) *Return to laughter*, New York, Harper and Row; reprinted 1964, New York, Doubleday.

BYNNER, J. and STRIBLEY, K. M. (eds) (1979) *Social research: principles and procedures*, London, Longman/The Open University Press. (Course Reader.)

COHEN, A. K. (1955) *Delinquent boys*, New York, Free Press. (2nd edn, 1971.)

COXON, A. and JONES, C. (1978) *The images of occupational prestige*, London, Macmillan.

CRESSEY, D. R. (1950) 'The criminal violation of financial trust', *American Sociological Review*, Vol. 15, December. (Set Reading; supplied as Supplementary Material.)

DAVIES, M. and KELLY, E. (1976) 'The social worker, the client and the social anthropologist', *British Journal of Social Work*, Vol. 6, No. 2, pp. 213–31.

DENZIN, N. K. (1971) 'The logic of naturalistic inquiry', *Social Forces*, Vol. 50, pp. 166–82. Reprinted in Bynner, J. and Stribley, K. M. (eds) (1979), Ch. 5.

DOUGLAS, J. D. (1972) *Research on deviance*, New York, Random House.

DOWNES, D. (1966) *The delinquent solution*, London, Routledge and Kegan Paul.

FREILICH, M. (1970) *Marginal natives*, New York, Harper and Row.

FURLONG, F. (1977) 'Anancy goes to school: a case study of pupils' knowledge of their teachers', in Woods, P. and Hammersley, M. (eds) (1977) *School experience*, London, Croom Helm.

GLASER, B. and STRAUSS, A. (1968) *The discovery of grounded theory*, London, Weidenfeld and Nicolson.

GOFFMAN, E. (1968a) *The presentation of self in everyday life*, Harmondsworth, Penguin.

GOFFMAN, E. (1968b) *Stigma: notes on the management of spoiled identity*, Harmondsworth, Penguin.

GOLDE, P. (1970) *Women in the field: anthropological experiences*, Chicago, Aldine.

HABENSTEIN, R. (1970) *Pathways to data*, Chicago, Aldine.

HAMMOND, P. (1964) *Sociologists at work*, New York, Basic Books.

HARGREAVES, D. H. (1967) *Social relations in a secondary school*, London, Routledge and Kegan Paul.

HARGREAVES, D. H., HESTER, S. K. and MELLOR, F. J. (1975) *Deviance in classrooms*, London, Routledge and Kegan Paul.

HUMPHREYS, L. (1970) *Tearoom trade*, London, Duckworth.

JENKINS, R. and MACRAE, J. (1967) 'Community polarisation in Northern Ireland', *International Peace Research Association*, Vol. 3, The Hague, Van Groeningen.

KRAIN, M. (1974) 'On staying loose in the army reserve', unpublished paper, University of Kansas.

LACEY, C. (1970) *Hightown Grammar*, Manchester, Manchester University Press.

LINDESMITH, A. (1947) *Opiate addiction*, New York, Principia Press.

LOFLAND, J. (1976) *Doing social life*, London, John Wiley and Sons.

MACINTYRE, S. (1977) *Single and pregnant*, London, Croom Helm.

MERTON, R. K. (1940) 'Fact and factitiousness in ethnic opinionnaires', *American Sociological Review*, Vol. 5, pp. 13–27.

POWDERMAKER, H. (1966) *Stranger and friend*, New York, Norton.

RUBINGTON, E. and WEINBERG, M. (1968) *Deviance: the interactionist perspective*, New York, Collier-Macmillan.

SHIPMAN, M. (ed.) (1976) *The organisation and impact of social research*, London, Routledge and Kegan Paul.

SPENCER, G. (1973) 'Methodological issues in the study of bureaucratic elites: a case study of West Point', *Social Problems*, Vol. 21, pp. 90–103.

SPINDLER, G. (1970) *Being an anthropologist*, London, Holt, Rinehart and Winston.

STONE, G. (1970) 'Appearance and the self', in Stone, G. and Faberman, H. (eds) (1976) *Social psychology through symbolic interactionism*, New York, Ginn-Blaisdell.

SUDNOW, D. (1965) 'Normal crimes: sociological features of the penal code in a Public Defender Office', *Social Problems*, Vol. 12, No. 3, Winter, pp. 255–76. (Set Reading; supplied as Supplementary Material.)

SUTHERLAND, E. H. (1949) *White collar crime*, New York, Dryden Press.

TAYLOR, I., WALTON, P. and YOUNG, J. (1973) *The new criminology*, London, Routledge and Kegan Paul.

VIDICH, A. J. and BENSMAN, J. (1958) *Small town in mass society*, Princeton, Princeton University Press.

VIDICH, A. J., BENSMAN, J. and STEIN, M. R. (eds) (1964) *Reflections on community studies*, New York, John Wiley and Sons.

WAX, R. (1971) *Doing fieldwork*, Chicago, University of Chicago Press.

WHYTE, W. F. (1955) *Street corner society*, 2nd edn, Chicago, University of Chicago Press.

WISEMAN, J. P. (1974) 'The research web', *Urban Life and Culture*, Vol. 3, pp. 317–28. Reprinted in Bynner, J. and Stribley, K. M. (eds) (1979), Ch. 10.

WOODS, P. (1979) *The divided school*, London, Routledge and Kegan Paul.

WOODS, P. (1976) 'Having a laugh', in Hammersley, M. and Woods, P. (eds) (1976) *The process of schooling*, London, Routledge and Kegan Paul.

	PICTURE VERSION	ORDINARY VERSION (Independent variable)	DIFFERENCE IN % (PICTURE/ ORDINARY)
STUDENTS PASSED (Dependent variable)	78·2	70·4	$+7·8 = d$
FAILED	21·8	29·6	$-7·8 = d$
Total	100% (N=54)	100% (N=55)	

Part 2   Two Variable Analysis
Prepared by Cathie Marsh for the Course Team

Block 6   Part 2

Contents

Aims

To make you familiar with quantitative data presented in tables, principally 2 by 2 tables. To teach you to distinguish between tables as storehouses of information and tables which present an analytical interpretation. To show how and when tables and variables may be collapsed as a means of simplification and clarification. To analyse the association in a table between two variables by using a statistic d and to calculate a confidence interval for d. The over-riding aim of this Part is to teach you how to draw conclusions from quantitative data for two variables.

Study Guide

There is no set or recommended reading for this Part.

Further Reading

EHRENBERG, A. S. C. (1975) *Data reduction*, London, John Wiley, Ch. 1.

LEOTHER, H. J. and McTAVISH, D. G. (1974) *Descriptive statistics for sociologists*, Boston, Allyn and Bacon, Ch. 7.

1 Introduction

1.1 This Part is devoted to constructing and reading *tables* – a process whose complexity is almost always underestimated. Putting figures into a table does not require any great statistical expertise, but it requires a great deal of thought to do well so that the reader of the table will be able to see at a glance what is going on. Throughout this Part the emphasis will be on deciding what any particular table means, what information about relationships can be obtained from it and how that information can be summarized.

table

1.2 Tables have two major jobs to do; they have to act both as a storehouse for the information that they contain while at the same time they have to be able to tell a clear story. Considerations of cost in printing enter very heavily into decisions about how to lay tables out and unfortunately this frequently leads to a very condensed format. Government publications of tables often perform the storehouse function much better than they tell a story. Consider Table 1, which is taken from the *Department of Employment Gazette* (May, 1977). It shows the movement in the Retail Price Index in the past few years. The entries in the cells of a table may be numbers (frequencies) or mean values of another variable. This is a table containing values of an index of average prices. Spend *only* one minute trying to determine the trend in the index of retail prices for seasonal food, all items and all items less seasonal food.

Table 1   Retail prices – United Kingdom: general index of retail prices

		ALL ITEMS	FOOD† All	Items the prices of which show significant seasonal variations	All items other than those the prices of which show significant seasonal variations	Items mainly manufactured in the United Kingdom — Primarily from home-produced raw materials	Primarily from imported raw materials	All	Items mainly home-produced for direct consumption	Items mainly imported for direct consumption	All items except food	All items except food the prices of which show significant seasonal variations
1974	Monthly averages	108·5	106·1	103·0	106·9	111·7	115·9	114·2	94·7	105·0	109·3	108·8
1975		134·8	133·3	129·8	134·3	140·7	156·8	150·2	116·9	120·9	135·3	135·1
1976		157·1	159·9	177·7	156·8	161·4	171·6	167·4	147·7	142·9	156·4	156·5
1974	November 12	115·2	113·3	105·7	115·0	121·9	130·3	126·9	97·2	110·4	115·8	115·6
	December 10	116·9	114·4	106·5	116·3	123·9	133·4	129·5	96·4	111·1	117·7	117·4
1975	January 14	119·9	118·3	106·6	121·1	128·9	143·3	137·5	98·1	113·3	120·4	120·5
	February 18	121·9	121·3	108·9	124·2	131·7	150·8	143·0	98·8	114·2	122·1	122·5
	March 18	124·3	126·0	114·9	128·7	133·1	153·7	145·3	108·9	116·9	123·8	124·8
	April 15	129·1	130·7	124·8	132·2	137·7	156·3	148·7	113·8	119·2	128·7	129·4
	May 13	134·5	132·7	129·4	133·8	139·3	158·4	150·6	115·3	120·2	135·0	134·8
	June 17	137·1	135·9	140·3	135·2	141·0	160·0	152·2	116·7	121·2	137·5	137·1
	July 15	138·5	136·3	140·2	135·7	143·0	160·6	153·4	115·9	121·4	139·2	138·5
	August 12	139·3	136·3	131·7	137·5	143·5	160·3	154·4	121·8	122·5	140·3	139·7
	September 16	140·5	137·3	133·8	138·3	144·6	160·0	153·7	123·0	122·6	141·5	140·9
	October 14	142·5	138·4	137·9	138·9	147·2	158·8	154·1	123·1	124·7	143·8	142·8
	November 11	144·2	141·6	140·1	142·4	148·9	158·5	154·6	133·1	126·5	145·0	144·5
	December 9	146·0	144·2	148·9	143·9	149·8	160·4	156·1	134·6	128·2	146·6	146·1
1976	January 13	147·9	148·3	158·6	146·6	151·2	162·4	157·8	137·3	132·4	147·9	147·6
	February 17	149·8	152·1	173·5	148·2	153·9	164·5	160·2	137·5	134·1	149·1	149·0
	March 16	150·6	153·8	181·2	148·6	154·3	165·0	160·6	138·0	134·4	149·8	149·5
	April 13	153·5	156·7	189·9	150·4	157·4	166·6	162·8	139·6	135·5	152·7	152·2
	May 18	155·2	157·1	184·8	151·9	157·9	167·6	163·6	141·3	137·9	154·7	154·2
	June 15	156·0	156·7	174·3	153·5	157·8	168·4	164·1	144·7	139·7	155·9	155·4
	July 13	156·3	153·4	149·0	154·8	160·3	169·6	165·8	145·6	140·6	157·2	156·8
	August 17	158·5	158·4	163·6	157·8	162·0	173·5	168·8	148·7	143·2	158·6	158·5
	September 14	160·6	164·4	178·6	161·9	163·8	175·5	170·7	157·2	146·5	159·5	160·0
	October 12	163·5	169·3	184·0	166·8	171·1	179·1	175·8	160·9	152·1	161·8	162·8
	November 16‖	165·8	172·7	192·8	169·1	172·6	182·2	178·3	160·2	157·4	163·8	164·8
	December 14‖	168·0	176·1	202·1	171·4	174·4	184·8	180·5	161·8	160·5	165·6	166·8
1977	January 18	172·4	183·1	214·8	177·1	178·7	189·7	185·2	169·6	165·7	169·3	170·9
	February 15	174·1	184·5	216·8	178·5	179·8	192·7	187·5	169·1	167·3	171·1	172·5
	March 15	175·8	186·5	215·7	181·0	185·1	197·8	192·7	168·9	167·9	172·6	174·3
	April 19	180·3	189·6	223·9	183·2	189·7	200·6	196·2	168·9	169·7	177·6	178·7

Source: *Department of Employment Gazette* (May, 1977) Table 132, p. 544

1.3 It is very hard to see quickly from Table 1 what has been happening to retail prices in recent years. The following *graph* (Figure 1) tells a much clearer story. It hits you between the eyes that the Index has been going up. But when you close

graph

Figure 1   Index of retail prices

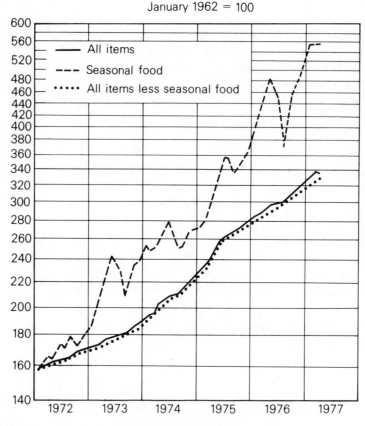

Source: Department of Employment Gazette (May, 1977) p. 547

the book and try to remember what the graph told you, will you remember any more than the fact that it went up? Probably not. And if you wanted to rework the figures in your own way, you would not be able to use the graph. So tables do have the advantage over graphs of being more precise and storing the information in a form that can be reworked. In this Part we shall concentrate on *frequency tables,* where the number in each cell represents the number of cases with certain characteristics.

frequency table

1.4   This Part will enable you to take a chunk of undigested figures, such as the ones in Table 1, and convert them into something as clear as the graph in Figure 1. We shall discuss some of the principles of good layout for tables, but you will often find that you need to apply these same rules to reconstruct and read an already existing table before you can use it for your purposes. We hope that by the end of this Part you will not be one of those people who reads a social science book, skipping over the tables when they crop up in the text. People include tables in their argument to allow the reader to check their conclusions personally; and far too often, on closer inspection of the tables in a text, errors or ambiguities of interpretation may become clear. It is very important that you should develop a skill for gutting a table of the information it contains, even if this involves reworking the table before you can 'read' it.

1.5   The most common mistake is to imagine that you can make sense of tabular information quickly, at a glance. The better laid out the table is, of course, the more possible this is, but when you are starting to gain experience, *take it slowly.* In an average-sized table there is so much information presented that it would probably take a page or two of text to express it in words. So you must expect to spend some time on getting the information from it; as you become more experienced at this you will find you get quicker at doing it (further reading on this topic: Ehrenberg, 1975, Ch. 1).

2 Defining a Few Terms

2.1 The *cases* that you put in a table can be people, households, industries, countries or virtually anything. When the cases are people who are interviewed, we often refer to them as *respondents*.

case

respondent

2.2 The table that is constructed of two variables is a way of showing the joint distribution of those variables. We do this by putting the information about one of the variables in the *rows*:

row

and the information about the other variable in the *columns*:

column

Each row and column usually has a total presented at the right-hand end and at the bottom respectively; these are called the *totals* or *marginals*. The grand total is also usually presented. Any figure which is the base for a percentage is labelled '*N*'.

marginal

2.3 The table is constructed by placing each individual case in the appropriate pigeonhole depending on the value that the case has on both of the variables. We call these pigeonholes the slightly more scientific name *cells* and the number in each cell is called the *cell frequency*.

cell frequency

Activity 1
This activity should take fifteen minutes.
Before we go on any further, just check that you are conversant with the way a table is constructed by doing this activity. We are going to spend a lot of time in the Part analysing a table derived from the Oxford Social Mobility Project.[1] Part of this study involved an interview survey of 10 309 men aged 20 to 64 and details of the respondents' current jobs and their fathers' jobs were obtained. Both respondents' and fathers' jobs were classified into seven different class categories. A table was then constructed (excluding agricultural workers and those for whom the details were missing) showing the breakdown of father's class by respondent's class.

Imagine that you are a research worker on the project and that the final results are just coming in. You have already put 8562 of the respondents into a table to show

---

[1] *For details of questions asked, coding scheme used and a discussion of some of the results, see Goldthorpe and Llewellyn (1977).*

father's class by respondent's class; this is what the table looks like so far (Table 2).

Table 2   Incomplete social mobility table

		Respondent's class							Total
		1	2	3	4	5	6	7	
Father's class	1	310	130	79	46	33	37	44	679
	2	161	128	66	33	53	58	47	546
	3	128	109	88	51	89	107	113	685
	4	123	128	81	187	88	133	144	884
	5	154	147	108	83	170	228	180	1 070
	6	201	227	215	165	319	789	659	2 575
	7	150	181	187	122	274	525	684	2 123
Total		1 227	1 050	824	687	1 026	1 877	1 871	N= 8 562
							+ Agricultural workers		859
							+ Missing cases		873
							Total sample size		10 294

(a)   How many cases are presented in Table 2?
How many rows are there?
What is the cell frequency for respondents in social class 3 with fathers in social class 5?

(b)   Table 3 gives the details of the last 15 respondents to fit into Table 2. Add them into Table 2 and make any adjustments to the row and column marginals, the grand total and the total sample size.

Table 3

Name[1]	Father's class	Own class
J. King	5	3
R. Nadathur	4	6
R. G. Buick	5	6
K. Rolfe	father dead	1
G. Newton	6	3
P. L. Godfreys	4	1
R. C. Joyce	6	7
D. Higgins	3	3
C. J. Jackson	7	1
W. Turner	not known	6
F. Stacey	7	6
F. Maddox	3	6
R. T. Maclaren	1	1
S. E. Houkes	2	6
L. P. Day	7	6

Note:
[1] Names entirely fictitious

2.4   What does a table such as the one you have just completed tell you that the original information about father's class and respondent's class alone does not tell you? We only had information about the distribution of each of the variables taken separately. Look at the marginals that you obtained for father's class and respondent's class from the table you have just constructed. We could show the information about respondent's class like Figure 2 and the information about father's class like Figure 3. A table tells us more than these two histograms would. When we know the *joint* distribution of the two variables, it is like being able to construct a histogram in three dimensions (Figure 4). This shows the joint

Figure 2   Frequency of respondent's class

Figure 3   Frequency of father's class

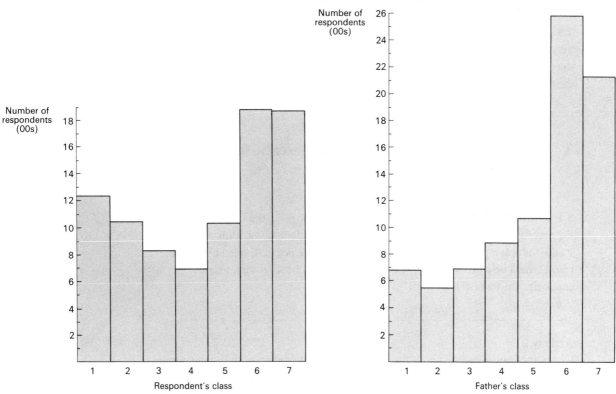

Figure 4   Three-dimensional histogram: cross-tabulation of Figures 2 and 3

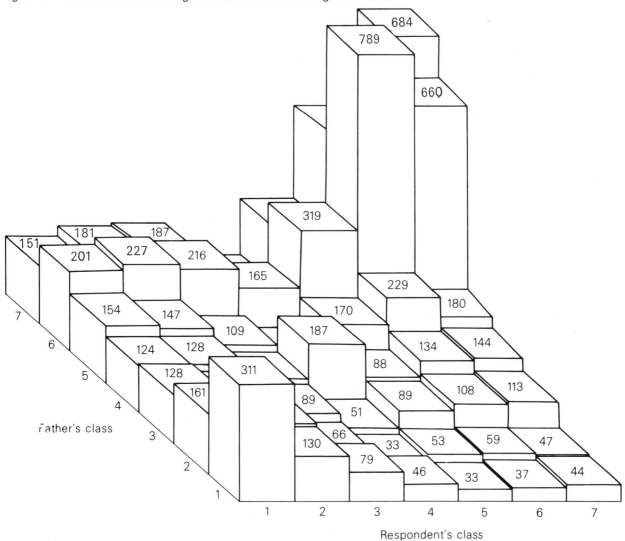

distribution of these two variables. Note that this figure is the *cross-tabulation* of Figures 2 and 3.

2.5 As you can see, showing the *joint distribution* of two variables in a table is only feasible when the number of categories in each variable is not great otherwise the table would be huge. This means that tabular presentation is not usually the most suitable form of displaying information recorded on interval scales.

joint distribution

3 Constructing Percentage Tables to Describe the Information Contained in 2 by 2 Tables

3.1 Now I shall reveal the first weapon at our disposal in the crusade for clarity: the percentage. Expressing x as a percentage of y is done by dividing x by the base y and multiplying the result by 100. If the result were not multiplied by 100, the result would be a proportion, so percentages and proportions are, loosely speaking, 'the same thing'.

Activity 2
Check that you are clear about the distinction by calculating both the percentage and proportion of the total of respondents in Activity 1 who were in social class 3 (use Table 4).

3.2 So the first thing that is usually done to any table is that the cell frequencies are converted into percentages. Why do you think this is necessary? If we look at the complete version of the mobility table that you completed we shall see why it is so difficult to read tables with only the *raw cell frequencies*.

raw cell frequency

Write a paragraph on why you think it is necessary to convert frequencies into percentages and compare your answer with paragraph 3.3. Spend two minutes doing this before proceeding.

3.3 I expect you found it very hard to make out what was being said in the mobility table. This is because none of the figures was expressed as a percentage and it is only when figures are expressed as percentages that they become comparable. Look at the first column which contains all those people who were in social class 1 when they were interviewed; there are 1230 such people. 311 of these had fathers who were also in social class 1, and 201 of them had fathers who were in social class 6. But these figures are not comparable, because in order to interpret these figures you have to remember that 311 is almost half of the total number of those with fathers in social class 1; in other words almost half of those who had fathers with top professional and managerial jobs obtained similar jobs themselves. But of 2577 with fathers in social class 6, only 201 ended up in social class 1.

3.4 So the table would have made much more sense if it had been presented in percentages, because then we could have seen what was going on. But the problem is: there are three alternative possibilities for presenting percentages; which do we choose?

Table 4   Complete social mobility table: raw cell frequencies

		Respondent's class							
		1	2	3	4	5	6	7	Total
Father's class	1	311	130	79	46	33	37	44	680
	2	161	128	66	33	53	59	47	547
	3	128	109	89	51	89	108	113	687
	4	124	128	81	187	88	134	144	886
	5	154	147	109	83	170	229	180	1 072
	6	201	227	216	165	319	789	660	2 577
	7	151	181	187	122	274	527	684	2 126
Total		1 230	1 050	827	687	1 026	1 883	1 872	N=8 575
						+ Agricultural workers			859
						+ Missing cases			875
						Total sample size			10 309

Source: Social Mobility Group, Nuffield College (1972) *Social mobility survey*
Note: A two-stage sample of male electors producing 10 309 usable interviews representing a response rate of 81.8 per cent

We can calculate each cell as a percentage of the grand total, as a percentage of its row marginal or as a percentage of its column marginal; so there are three possible totals on which a percentage can be based.

Examine Tables 5, 6 and 7, and make notes saying whether you think that the method of calculating the percentages makes useful sense of the information contained in each of the tables. Then compare your notes with the discussion in paragraph 3.5.

Table 5   Social mobility table: total percentages

		Respondent's class							
		1	2	3	4	5	6	7	Total %
Father's class	1	3.6	1.5	0.9	0.5	0.4	0.4	0.5	7.9
	2	1.9	1.5	0.8	0.4	0.6	0.7	0.5	6.4
	3	1.5	1.3	1.0	0.6	1.0	1.3	1.3	8.0
	4	1.4	1.5	0.9	2.2	1.0	1.6	1.7	10.3
	5	1.8	1.7	1.3	1.0	2.0	2.7	2.1	12.5
	6	2.3	2.6	2.5	1.9	3.7	9.2	7.7	30.1
	7	1.8	2.1	2.2	1.4	3.2	6.1	8.0	24.8
Total %		14.3	12.2	9.6	8.0	12.0	22.0	21.8	100 N=8 575

Source: See Table 4

Table 6   Social mobility table: column percentages

		Respondent's class							
		1	2	3	4	5	6	7	Total %
Father's class	1	25.3	12.4	9.6	6.7	3.2	2.0	2.4	7.9
	2	13.1	12.2	8.0	4.8	5.2	3.1	2.5	6.4
	3	10.4	10.4	10.8	7.4	8.7	5.7	6.0	8.0
	4	10.1	12.2	9.8	27.2	8.6	7.1	7.7	10.3
	5	12.5	14.0	13.2	12.1	16.6	12.2	9.6	12.5
	6	16.4	21.7	26.1	24.0	13.1	41.8	35.2	30.1
	7	12.2	17.1	22.6	17.8	26.7	28.0	36.6	24.8
Total %		100 (N=1 230)	100 (N=1 050)	100 (N=827)	100 (N=687)	100 (N=1 026)	100 (N=1 883)	100 (N=1 872)	100 (N=8 575)

Source: See Table 4

Table 7   Social mobility table: row percentages

		\multicolumn{8}{c}{Respondent's class}							
		1	2	3	4	5	6	7		Total %
Father's class	1	47.7	19.1	11.6	6.8	4.9	5.4	6.5	100	(N=680)
	2	29.4	23.3	12.1	6.0	9.7	10.8	8.6	100	(N=547)
	3	18.6	15.9	13.0	7.4	13.0	15.7	16.4	100	(N=687)
	4	14.0	14.4	9.1	21.1	9.9	15.1	16.3	100	(N=886)
	5	14.4	13.7	10.2	7.7	15.9	21.4	16.8	100	(N=1 072)
	6	7.8	8.8	8.4	6.4	12.4	30.6	25.6	100	(N=2 577)
	7	7.1	8.5	8.8	5.7	12.9	24.8	32.2	100	(N=2 126)
Total %		14.3	12.2	9.6	8.0	12.0	22.0	21.8	100	(N=8 575)

Source: See Table 4

3.5   The first format (Table 5) is not much use to anybody. Each of the figures in the cells has been individually expressed as a percentage of the grand total 8575. So we know how the 7.9 per cent of the total, i.e. people whose fathers were in social class 1 are distributed throughout the occupational structure, but we cannot compare these figures with the ones in the next row, i.e. those people whose fathers were in social class 2, until we remember that these only add up to 6.4 per cent of the total. Since no direct comparison can be made in a table like this, percentages of the grand total are rarely used.

3.6   Table 6 expresses the figures in each cell as a percentage of the total in that column; that is, every figure is expressed as a percentage of the total number of people in that class of *respondents*. Just glance down column 4. What this tells you is that of the 687 people who were in social class 4:

    6.7% of them had fathers in social class 1
    4.8% of them had fathers in social class 2
    7.4% of them had fathers in social class 3
    27.2% of them had fathers in social class 4
    12.1% of them had fathers in social class 5
    24.0% of them had fathers in social class 6
    17.8% of them had fathers in social class 7

In other words, it tells you where people in the same social class now come from. And these figures can be directly compared with, say, the breakdown of backgrounds of those in social class 7, by looking down the 7th column. We can say that whereas 6.7 per cent of people now in social class 4 had fathers from social class 1, only 2.4 per cent of people now in social class 7 had fathers in this top managerial category.

3.7   It does not matter that the totals in each case are different, that there are 687 people in social class 4 and 1872 in social class 7, for we have standardized this by expressing it as a percentage of the total number in the particular class.

What would you conclude from Table 6:

(a) by reading along the whole of the top row, as the eye moves from social class 1 to 7;

(b) by reading similarly along the bottom?

Spend five minutes answering these before proceeding.

a) Far less likely when father SC 1 to get son SC 7 — a common.

b) a similar reversal

3.8 We can conclude, by reading along the whole of the top row, that as the eye moves from those presently in social class 1 to those presently in social class 7 you can see that respondents become less likely to have had a father in social class 1. Similarly, by reading along the bottom row, we can conclude that more or less the opposite is true.

3.9 So *column* percentages are useful for making comparisons along *rows*. Goldthorpe and Llewellyn (1977) call this an 'inflow mobility matrix' since it tells you where the present incumbents of the social classes came from; they use it to examine the different composition of each of the social classes according to the class origins of the respondents. For example, they show that social class 1 has a much wider basis of recruitment than many people previously had thought. But of course, as they point out, one could compare each of the figures in the first row with the total row percentage, which is 7.9 for social class 1. If there was perfect social mobility then every single figure in the row would be round about 7.9 per cent also. But we can see clearly by glancing along that top row that the figures range far from 7.9. To the extent that they depart from the figure that we might 'expect' to find, we say that there is *association* in the table; knowledge of father's class allows us to improve prediction of son's class.

association

3.10 But we might wish to make comparisons between columns, i.e. between different classes of origins. Goldthorpe and Llewellyn also present this table, using the same data but presenting row percentages instead of column percentages, and they call this an 'outflow mobility table', since it allows you to compare the different fortunes of sons of the different occupational groupings (Table 7). Note that these are not all at one point in time, however. So when we look at Table 7 which presents row percentages, we can get an idea of the second generation movement of different classes. Instead of discovering that 25 per cent of people in social class 1 had fathers in social class 1, we discover that 48 per cent of fathers in social class 1 had sons who also ended up in similar managerial jobs. Where does the discrepancy come from? Why are these figures not the same? Part of the reason is because different social classes have different numbers of children, but the main reason is because the class composition of the occupational structure has changed in the generation considered: there are now almost double the proportion engaged in these sorts of jobs as there were a generation ago, so you could not expect to find the same figures.

3.11 So now we know that you get different information from row percentages and column percentages. We know that if you make all the columns add up to 100 per cent then you extract the relevant information by reading along the rows, and looking to see if any of the figures is far from the total percentage of that row. Similarly, if we made all the rows add up to 100 per cent then we read the table by looking systematically down the columns, and comparing each figure with the column percentage. Finally, we should always check that none of the percentages mentioned are based on a very small figure. A good rule of thumb is not to present percentages when the base *N* is less than 20, but report the frequencies involved in a footnote so that the original table can be reconstructed.

Activity 3

Table 8, below, is adapted from Chapter 5 of Fiegehen (1977) *Poverty and progress in Britain 1953–73*. In this book, the author is concerned to discover what are the causes of poverty in order to give advice to policy-makers about the type of social policy that would best alleviate poverty.

One of the things that he wished to discover was whether household size has any effect on whether the family is poor or not. He re-analysed some data originally collected for the Family Expenditure Survey and got a table something like Table 8.

Table 8   Households in poverty by size of household

Number in household	In poverty	Not in poverty	Total
1	259	991	1 250
2	148	2 159	2 307
3	45	1 319	1 364
4	21	1 272	1 293
5	16	573	589
6	8	206	214
7	9	84	93
8	4	34	38
Total	510	6 638	7 148

(a)   Try running the percentages both ways and write a paragraph about what each of the ways tells you about the relationship between poverty and household size.

(b)   What advice would you give to a policy-maker about where to concentrate resources to alleviate poverty on the basis of these figures?

4   Constructing Percentage Tables to Test Causal Hypotheses

4.1   Up to now we have been discussing tables that have been purely descriptive; we have talked about how to percentage the information to get the maximum amount of clarity from it. We have seen that row percentages and column percentages describe rather different aspects of the same table, and that one would choose one in preference to the other because of the type of information one wanted to concentrate on.

4.2   But tabular information is also presented by social scientists who want to test a hypothesis that an *independent variable* is having an effect on a *dependent variable*. When this is the case (as it most often is), then there is a rule to be applied, as we shall see. Check the glossary to remind yourself of the terms independent and dependent variable.

independent variable, dependent variable

4.3   Let us take a hypothetical example; let us suppose that we wanted to establish whether additional pictorial illustrations would help people learn statistics more easily. We might proceed by splitting all the people doing Blocks 6 and 7 of this course (let us suppose there were 109 such people) into two random halves, giving one half the course texts as they are now, and giving the other half a new version with at least one picture on every page. Our hypothesis would be that the group who were given the pictorial version would do better than the group who got the present version. We would expect more of them to gain a credit on the course as our operational definition of 'do better'. We could model our hypothesis like this; the arrow from 'version of the text' to 'success at statistics' shows that we think the former has some *causal* effect on the latter (Figure 5).

Figure 5

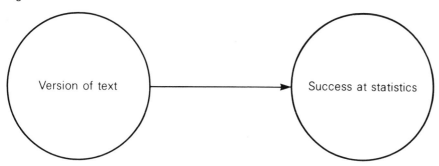

4.4   Let us imagine that, at the end of the course, we discovered the following results (Table 9).

Table 9   Imaginary teaching methods experiment: raw cell frequencies

	Picture version	Ordinary version	Total
Passed	50	31	81
Failed	4	24	28
Total	54	55	N=109

Which way do we want to calculate the percentages? Do we want to compare differently taught groups with respect to their pass rates or do we want to compare different pass rate groups in terms of their method of teaching? This is quite a tricky question, so think carefully, calculate both sets of percentages, say which table makes which comparisons and decide which one you think is most useful. Then read paragraphs 4.5 and 4.6.

Row %   P.V.   O.V.
  P   62   38   100   → Compares Pass rates with their technique
  F   14   86   100

Col %.   PV   OV.
  P   93 | 56   → Compares technique with pass rates.
  F   7 | 44
         100 | 100.

Col % most useful.

4.5   In this example we are trying to assess the effect that different ways of presenting statistical texts have on the students' understanding of the material, as measured by the pass rate. For this reason we should pick the version of the table which enables us to compare differently taught groups (the independent variable) with regard to their pass rates (the dependent variable). So long as the marginals on the dependent variable are representative of the population from which they come, whenever we want to consider the effect of a causally prior independent variable on a dependent variable we percentage within categories of the independent variable. We want to be able to look at the percentage of the differently taught groups who passed, rather than the percentage of those who came from a particular group. It might be worth memorizing the following rule:

> *Make the categories of the independent variable add up to 100 per cent;*
> *then read the table by comparing the percentages across categories of the*
> *dependent variable.*

4.6   It does not matter too much whether the dependent variable is in the rows or columns, although you will find it easier to remember what you are doing if you get into the habit of always doing the same thing. (The summary chart, Appendix 1, at the end of this Part will help you with the practicalities of table layout.) The important thing is that you calculate the right percentages. The result should look like Table 10.

Table 10   Imaginary teaching methods experiment: percentage table

		Independent variable		Difference in % (picture/ordinary)
		Picture version	Ordinary version	
Dependent variable	Passed	92.6	56.4	+36.2
	Failed	7.4	43.6	−36.2
Total		100% (N=54)	100% (N=55)	

4.7   Notice that I have not presented the totals of the passed and failed categories in the right-hand column. Instead I have calculated the difference in the percentages when you subtract the percentage who passed or failed among those with the ordinary version of the textbook from those who passed or failed among those with the pictorial version, i.e. I calculated percentage differences between the two levels or values of the independent variable.

4.8   So we would conclude that the picture version was probably having some effect, as a much higher proportion of those who had been taught with that version obtained the credit for the course. In fact, to be more precise about it, there is a large (36.2 per cent) difference between the groups who were taught with the picture version and those who were taught with the ordinary version.

Activity 4

Aronson and Mills[2] performed an experiment once as part of a larger research project with the central hypothesis that people come to love the things for which they have to suffer. They operationalized this by hypothesizing that groups with difficult initiation procedures would be more attractive to their members than groups which had no initiation conditions at all. In order to test this hypothesis, they divided a group of college students, all female, into test groups and a control group. They told them that they were taking part in an experimental discussion of sexual habits and that they would have to be prepared to talk about sex.

[2] *Fuller details in Aronson and Carlsmith (1968).*

However, some of the students also had to undergo what the authors call 'severe' initiation procedures before they were told they had been accepted to take part in this discussion. They had to stand up and read aloud to the researcher passages of very florid prose describing sexual activity. So this group were thought to have 'suffered' for admission to the group. Then all subjects were told that, since it was their first day, they would just be allowed to listen to one of the discussions through headphones. They would not be allowed to participate. Then all subjects listened to exactly the same pre-recorded (very boring) discussion of the sex habits of animals. After this they were asked how much they liked the sound of the group they were about to join. I have changed the results a lot in order to simplify the situation; imagine that they looked like Table 11.

Table 11   Adapted Aronson and Mills's results: raw cell frequencies

	No initiation	Severe initiation	Total
Liked group	27	38	65
Did not like group	23	12	35
Total	50	50	$N=100$

Do you think that these results back-up the original hypothesis?

5   Collapsing Tables

5.1   A table, as we said before, is often having to perform two jobs at once: (a) to store information, and (b) to present it clearly. These two jobs often pull the researcher in opposite directions; if the greatest amount of information is to be stored then you will want to keep the maximum number of categories in your variables, whereas if the aim is to present it clearly then you will want to *collapse* or shorten the number of categories you present.

collapse

5.2   So we come to the second of the tools in our armoury for reducing the amount of data that are presented and clarifying the story that is told. (The first was the use of the percentage.) Reducing the number of categories in the variables is achieved by collapsing the numbers of rows or columns in a table. (You have come across this before in Block 5, Part 1 where categories in the smoking example were collapsed.) Thus we talk about collapsing tables when what we are really doing is collapsing or reducing the number of categories in one or other of the variables. This is really nothing more than re-coding the data at a slightly later stage in the analysis. (If you want to refresh your mind about *coding* at this stage, look back to Block 5, Part 1.) In the beginning, when the researcher is designing the questionnaire and the pre-coded responses, it is imperative to err on the side of caution in allowing separate categories for less common replies. Later on, when one knows how many people came under each category, one can make decisions about what to collapse.

coding

5.3   The same information can be collapsed in different ways to reveal different patterns. In a survey I was once involved with,[3] we asked respondents who had recently been involved in an industrial dispute what that dispute had primarily been about. It was an open-ended question, so the interviewers wrote down

---

[3] *Social Science Research Council Survey Unit: Multipurpose Survey, June, 1975.*

verbatim whatever the respondent said. In the preliminary stages of coding, we reduced the replies to eleven codes:

1   General complaints about pay, amount of pay
2   Complaints specifically about the method of payment, e.g. regularity
3   Promotion, promotion prospects
4   Hours worked, their convenience and length
5   Job insecurity, short-time working, redundancy threat
6   Personal relationships with people at work
7   Safety, health, physical conditions at work
8   Fringe benefits, holidays, etc.
9   Complaints about job content, inefficient machinery, etc.
10 Worked too hard, pace too fast
11 Sympathy action in support of some other group of workers

We also coded, as separate variables, whether the respondent used words such as 'unfair' or 'unjust' in presenting the reasons for a dispute and we also coded any references to the search for higher status. I think that by the time we had finished we had preserved a large amount of the richness of the original responses and in a relatively rigorous format. Our coding system functioned well as a storehouse of information but was too unwieldy to tell a very clear story.

5.4   Depending on your theoretical interest, you would choose to collapse this variable in different ways. Industrial sociologists often distinguish rewards and dissatisfactions that come from the work itself and those which are a by-product of work – such as pay and holidays. If you were concerned to distinguish between reasons for disputes in this way, you might decide to call 1, 2, 4, 5 and 8 by-products-of-work reasons and call 3, 6, 7, 9 and 10 work-itself reasons. You would then add these categories together and probably exclude category 11 all together because it did not fit in either of the new categories.

5.5   If, on the other hand, you were particularly interested in the background to workers becoming conscious about safety at work, you might be satisfied just to compare those who gave code 7 as an answer to everyone else, to see if there were any major differences. In that case, you would add up all the other categories apart from 7 and end up with a *dichotomous variable* that gives information about whether the cause of a dispute was the safety conditions or not. So we begin to see that the first principle guiding coding decisions will be one's research interests: decisions must be made that allow you to continue to answer the questions that interest you.

dichotomous variable

5.6   Let us now go back to Table 4, the social mobility table, and see if we can see any way in which the number of rows and columns could be cut down. This will involve having a closer look at the variable 'social class' than we have done up to now. Goldthorpe and Llewellyn (1977) tell us that the seven categories that they present in their tables are themselves the result of a previous classification having been collapsed. Originally the respondents' jobs were coded quite finely on a scale of occupational prestige; this scale was itself collapsed to yield the following categories:

1   Higher-grade professionals whether self-employed or salaried; higher-grade administrators and officials; and managers of large enterprises
2   Lower-grade professionals and higher-grade technicians; lower-grade administrators and officials; and managers of small enterprises
3   Routine non-manual workers and sales personnel
4   Small proprietors and self-employed artisans
5   Lower-grade technicians whose work is to some extent of a manual character; supervisors over manual workers
6   Skilled manual workers in industry
7   Semi-skilled and unskilled manual workers in industry

What we have to ask is whether this amount of detail is necessary for us to understand what is going on in the table. Goldthorpe and Llewellyn found it necessary to present that amount of detail but we might only be interested in looking at the manual/non-manual distinction to see how many people cross *this* divide through inter-generational mobility.

5.7 Let us try to reduce Table 4 so that it contains information only about those who crossed the manual/non-manual boundary line. It is important, when collapsing tables, to work from the raw figures and then to recalculate the percentages. We must first establish which of the categories are manual and which are non-manual jobs. In order to do this, we shall be forced to rely on conventional practice quite a lot; in truth, there are not many jobs that require only manual dexterity and no intellectual input, not many jobs that do not require the ability to read. As I sit here typing these words I am reminded of the necessity for those who write to have the manual skill of typing. But the authors' defence of their subdivisions according to manual/non-manual would be that moving from a skilled manual job to an unskilled clerical job is perceived as upward mobility by a large number of people in the population, because it crosses this conventional distinction between work on the shop-floor and work in the office; the pay may be less but the classification scheme they use was endorsed by a sample of people as being a reasonable reflection of the perceived social structure.

5.8 What are we going to do with the self-employed? We notice that code 4 does not include all the self-employed, because owners of the really big companies are already included in code 1. What is left is a large number of plumbers, electricians, decorators and so on. One could take the view that these jobs are themselves manual jobs if performed by people in employment, so we should collapse code 4 in with manual. But there will also be some small shop-keepers in here as well, who we would prefer to place in the non-manual category; however it is too late now for us to redivide the contents of code 4.

5.9 We do not have the information to redivide the category. If we had the original questions we could have partitioned the jobs into the categories we wanted. We might decide to exclude them altogether and present a table excluding the small artisans. This, however, would involve exclusion of 16 per cent of our cases and would therefore not be commendable. Let us agree to put code 4 in with codes 5, 6 and 7. So let us go back to Table 4 which presented the original figures. We can draw dashed lines across our table to show where to collapse and to do the necessary addition (Table 12), and thus we end up with Table 13.

Table 12   Complete social mobility table: raw cell frequencies showing where to collapse

| | | Respondent's class | | | | | | | |
		1	2	3	4	5	6	7	Total
	1	311	130	79	46	33	37	44	680
	2	161	128	66	33	53	59	47	547
	3	128	109	89	51	89	108	113	687
Father's class	4	124	128	81	187	88	134	144	886
	5	154	147	109	83	170	229	180	1 072
	6	201	227	216	165	319	789	660	2 577
	7	151	181	187	122	274	527	684	2 126
Total		1 230	1 050	827	687	1 026	1 883	1 872	N=8 575

Source: See Table 4

Table 13   Collapsed social mobility table: raw cell frequencies

| | | Respondent's class | | |
		Non-manual	Manual	Total
Father's class	Non-manual	1 201	713	1 914
	Manual	1 906	4 755	6 661
	Total	3 107	5 468	$N=8\,575$

Source: See Table 4

5.10   Going back to our first weapon of data reduction, the percentage, we can show what this table is telling us. Suppose we are interested in outflow mobility. Let us calculate percentages within categories of father's class (Table 14). Even

Table 14   Collapsed social mobility: percentage table

| | | Respondent's class | | |
		Non-manual	Manual	Total
Father's class	Non-manual	62.7	37.3	100% ($N=1\,914$)
	Manual	28.6	71.4	100% ($N=6\,661$)
	Difference in % (non-manual/manual)	+34.1	−34.1	
			Total	$N=8\,575$

Source: See Table 4

this table contains redundant information; once we know that 62.7 per cent of a dichotomized variable is non-manual, then it is automatically true that 37.3 per cent is manual. So we might have presented this table simply with the first column of information thus, Table 15. We can see at a glance now that there is a huge

Table 15   Social mobility percentage table collapsed even further

		% of respondents in non-manual jobs
Father's class	Non-manual	62.7 ($N = 1\,914$)
	Manual	28.6 ($N = 6\,661$)
	Difference in % (non-manual/manual)	+ 34.1
		Total $N = 8\,575$

Source: See Table 4

discrepancy in the proportions of people in non-manual jobs whose fathers had non-manual jobs as compared with those whose fathers had manual jobs. If crossing the manual/non-manual boundary is subjectively important to people, then we can see that only a relatively small proportion of manual workers achieve it.

5.11   Another way to think of the percentage difference is as a slope. We could have presented the results as two bar charts (Figure 6). We can see from this diagram that 34.1 per cent represents the increase in proportion of those with non-manual fathers as you move from manual to non-manual fathers. You can think of it as the amount one variable increases when you go from one category to another of another variable.

Figure 6   Two bar charts presenting the percentage difference as a slope

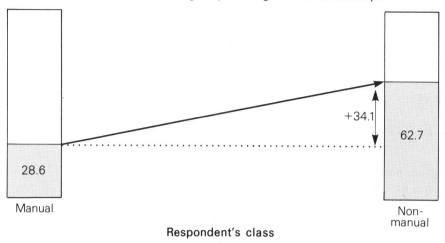

Respondent's class

☐ = Proportion with fathers in non-manual jobs

5.12   Are there any other rules governing the way in which decisions about collapsing categories should be made? The level of measurement should give you some guide.

Write a note on how you would use information about the level of measurement, in order to help you to make decisions about where to collapse variables.

5.13   With *nominal scales,* you can choose to collapse any category with any other, the only guidance being the question one is trying to answer by so doing. With *ordinal scales* where the numbers have no real meaning except to show that one code is smaller or larger than another, often one would collapse in order to give approximately equal numbers in each of the new categories. For example, suppose a sample of adult respondents in the UK were asked to rate their satisfaction with their locality as a place to live on a scale where 0 represents respondents extremely dissatisfied and 7 is extremely satisfied, they respond like this (Table 16). One might decide to call 6 and 7 'most satisfied', 4 and 5 'medium satisfied' and anything below 4 'least satisfied'. If the scale is an *interval scale,* one might decide to collapse below and above the mean or the median; however, tables are usually a wasteful way of presenting interval scale data. And of course, with ordinal and interval scales one should only collapse adjacent categories; you cannot add those who said 5 in response to the satisfaction question with those who said 8 without also including those who responded 6 or 7.

nominal scale

ordinal scale

interval scale

Table 16

Scale	1	2	3	4	5	6	7	Total
Cases	10	8	29	38	47	44	51	227

5.14 If your sample was stratified and contained different sampling fractions in different strata, it might be misleading to collapse the two strata together. The resulting percentages calculated would not be representative of any group in the population as a whole. For example, if you had selected a sample to give you equal proportions of employed and unemployed people, adding these groups together and saying that 25 per cent lived in council housing would be pretty meaningless – 25 per cent of what?

Activity 5
When a random sample of adults in the urban parts of the United Kingdom were asked in 1973 what religion they were, this is how they described themselves:

None, atheist, humanist	81
Jewish	5
Roman Catholic	108
Church of England/Scotland	621
'Mainline' non-conformist	
(Methodist, Baptist, Congregationalist, United Reform, Quakers)	97
'Fringe' non-conformist	
(millenarian/fundamentalist sects, Pentecostal, Jehovah's	
Witnesses, Christian Scientist, Mormon, Salvation Army, etc.)	14
Greek or Russian Orthodox	2
Oriental (Muslim, Buddhist, Hindu)	2
Agnostic	26
No answer or 'don't know'	10

$$N = 966$$

Would you have grouped the religions together in the same way? Collapse this variable down to the four categories that you think make most sense if you were looking to see if religion had any effect on voting behaviour.

5.15 Now a word of warning about collapsing tables: *It is a one-way process.* If you do decide to collapse your table to make it better at its story-telling job, do include the fuller version of the table in an appendix so that others coming after you can collapse it a different way if they so choose.

5.16 Second word of warning about collapsing tables: *different collapses give you different results.* Let me illustrate this with an example. Consider this table of satisfaction with locality by sex. (I was interested in finding the answer to the question: Are women more satisfied than men with the place where they live?) First I collapsed satisfaction into the three categories suggested in paragraph 5.13, cross-tabulated the results by sex and obtained the following, Table 17. But if I now decide I want to collapse satisfaction even further, I must either put the low with the medium or the high with the medium. Putting the low with the medium and calculating the percentages within the categories of sex (for sex is the independent variable here) I get Table 18. But if I put the high with the medium I get Table 19.

Table 17   Cross-tabulation of satisfaction with district by sex

	Satisfaction with district			
	Low (1–3)	Medium (4, 5)	High (6, 7)	Total
Male	61	72	10	143
Female	34	13	37	84
Total	95	85	47	$N = 227$

Table 18   One way of collapsing Table 17

| | Satisfaction with district | | Total |
	Low (1–5) (%)	High (6–7) (%)	
Male	133 (93.0)	10 (7.0)	N=143 (100%)
Female	47 (56.0)	37 (44.0)	N= 84 (100%)
Difference in % (male/female)	+37.0	−37.0	

Table 19   Another way of collapsing Table 17

| | Satisfaction with district | | Total |
	Low (1–3) (%)	High (4–7) (%)	
Male	61 (42.7)	82 (57.3)	N=143 (100%)
Female	34 (40.5)	50 (59.5)	N= 84 (100%)
Difference in % (male/female)	+2.2	−2.2	

5.17   The first collapse (Table 18) made it look as if women were very much more satisfied with their locality than men. But the second collapse (Table 19) seemed to tell us that there was not much difference.

Which is true? Write down your answers and then compare them with paragraph 5.18.

Neither, depend where you draw the line!

5.18   Neither of the collapsed tables is more true than the other. The 'truth' of the matter was contained in the first, fuller version, Table 17. First of all look at that original table holding a piece of paper over the medium category. Almost all the men were low, whereas under half of the women were low; so without the medium category, men were less satisfied. But now look also at the information in the medium category; almost half the men were in this category, whereas under one-sixth of the women were. So if you decide that medium is best put in with high, then this information counteracts the previous information that men were less satisfied. If on the other hand you decide that medium is more like low, then you get further confirmation that men are less satisfied.

5.19   I would probably argue that the first way of collapsing Table 17 is better from the point of view of telling the story, even though it leaves us with rather uneven marginals (180 and 47 as opposed to 95 and 132, Table 18). But there are no hard and fast rules here, so think very carefully about how to make the most appropriate decision about collapsing a table. You do not necessarily have to collapse any table.

5.20   You should bear the following points in mind; other things being equal:

(a)   try to get the marginals fairly equal;

(b)   with ordinal scales, for a 2 by 2 table consider collapsing above and below the median;

(c)   with an interval scale, consider collapsing above and below the mean; and

(d)   always present the results of obvious alternatives if they show very different results.

6   Reading the Information in a Percentage Table

6.1   Tables, as we have already noted, can be used both to convey information descriptively and to provide the information necessary to test a causal hypothesis. You should now be able to take any table and reduce it to a sensible percentage table. Up to now, we have not been able to avoid talking about what the tables are saying, describing and demonstrating. There are difficulties when trying to assess exactly what different tables do mean and we shall discuss a couple of the most important now.

6.2   Look back to Table 10 which showed the results of the hypothetical experiment, testing pictorial texts in comparison with ordinary ones. We concluded that, since a much higher proportion of those who had been taught with the picture version were successful, it was probably having some effect. We might have been happier if the results had looked like this, Table 20.

Refer back to Table 10

Table 20   Teaching methods experiment: one possible outcome

	Picture version	Ordinary version	Difference in % (picture/ordinary)
Passed	100.0	0.0	+100.0
Failed	0.0	100.0	−100.0
Total	100% (N=54)	100% (N=55)	

6.3   If *all* the people who got the new version passed and all those who got the old version failed (and this happened whatever group of people we tried it on so we could be sure it was not just a sampling fluke) then we would be justified in concluding that the type of course book offered was the only cause of whether a particular student passed or failed. In stricter, more philosophical language, we could say that having the pictorial version of the course text was both a sufficient and a necessary precondition of passing the exam.

6.4   Now for the bad news! You will almost certainly never come across a table like the one above in your whole encounter with social science. There are no relationships between two variables which produce a table like this, because there are no two sociological variables known to us where one is the complete single cause of the other. When we ask a question such as 'What causes some students to pass and others to fail?', we do not expect to be given one simple reply like 'The textbook they use'. Instead, we expect there to be a large number of factors involved. There are many aspects of the student's ability, motivation and situation to be taken into account, as well as many factors connected with the teaching. Worse still, these factors themselves may be associated with each other and therefore difficult to separate out.

6.5   You must brace yourself for small causal effects. The 36.2 per cent difference we encountered in the first version (Table 10) is, in fact, by social science standards, really quite large. We might have found a table like this (Table 21).

Table 21   Teaching methods experiment: another possible outcome

	Picture version	Ordinary version	Difference in % (picture/ordinary)
Passed	78.2	70.4	+ 7.8
Failed	21.8	29.6	− 7.8
Total	100% (N=54)	100% (N=55)	

6.6   Now the difference between the two groups is only 7.8 per cent. If we were to get results like this whenever we tried this experiment, on randomized groups of students, we would conclude that the version of the course textbook did indeed have an effect on the pass rate but that effect was very small, and that many other factors also influenced the pass rate.

6.7   Notice that I have not raised the question that the results might anyway not be representative of the population from which the sample was drawn. I have always asked you to imagine that these results were obtained over and over again so that one could be sure that the results were *not* the fluke of one sample. In Part 3 of this Block you will be told how to take into account the fact that you may only have one sample result from which to draw inferences about a population.

6.8   So we must be prepared to find small causal effects and not to expect all-or-nothing evidence of our causal hypotheses. But there is an even bigger difficulty when assessing whether the information in a particular table corroborates or rejects a causal hypothesis; we may not know whether the observed association is indeed evidence of a *cause* at all. One little phrase you would do well to memorize and remember whenever you read results of research is:

Correlation does not mean causation.

6.9   There is only one situation in which you can draw causal conclusions from the results with certainty: when you have done an experiment. (You can only call something an experiment when you have manipulated the independent variable yourself.) The example that we considered of the effect of textbooks on learning ability as measured by ability to pass exams was an experiment. When we found a difference in percentages of 36.2 per cent between the group with the pictorial text and the group with the ordinary text, we could conclude that it was something about the pictorial text that caused the difference in pass rate. Assuming that picking two different groups at random had had the desired effect of creating exactly similar groups before they started, the only thing that had happened differently to the groups was that one had a pictorial text and the other an ordinary one.

6.10   Let us illustrate this with an example from voting behaviour. Suppose you were a sociologist who suspected that the kind of jobs that people did had an effect on the way in which they voted. If you wished to conduct an experiment, you would have to take a sample of people at the age of 18, split them randomly into two groups, *make* one group do manual jobs and the other group do non-manual jobs, and then, perhaps ten years later, look to see if this had had any effect on the way in which they voted; any differences in their voting behaviour would have been due to the experimental manipulation. (These ideas should be familiar to you after their treatment in the course so far. If you find any difficulty with them, check the glossary entry for references to *experiment*.)   **experiment**

6.11   Very often, social scientists are forced to use already existing variation from which to draw inferences about causality. Drawing conclusions from tables which contain non-experimental data is always a process of saying 'If we can assume that variable *x* is causally prior to variable *y*, and if we can assume that there is nothing else that we have not controlled which might have a causal effect on both variables systematically, then and only then can we conclude that x has a causal effect on y'.

6.12   But, of course, an experiment with people's lives in this way is not only totally impracticable but also ethically quite unjustifiable. What most sociologists investigating this problem have used is survey material relating to the two factors. You would pick a random sample of voters and then perhaps interview them to collect information about the jobs that they did and the way in which they voted; then, once the results had been coded, you would cross-tabulate vote by type of job and see if there was any evidence for your causal hypothesis being true. Suppose that the results looked like this (Table 22).

Table 22   Cross-tabulation of job by vote

	Non-manual %	Manual %	Difference in % (non-manual/manual)
Conservative	45	22	23
Liberal	24	17	7
Labour	18	47	− 29
Other	1	1	0
Don't know	12	13	− 1
Total	100% (N=489)	100% (N=913)	

Source: Adapted from Runciman (1972). Survey of 1 402 electors in England and Wales drawn in a two stage random sample, 1962.

Could you conclude from Table 22 that the type of job carried out affects the way people vote?

6.13   We can see that the percentage of people voting for any of the parties is not the same in the non-manual column as it is in the manual column; some of the differences in percentages are quite large. So we conclude that there is 'something going on'; expressing it more scientifically, the fact that the percentages are different tells us that vote is related to the kind of job you do. These two variables are *associated*.

6.14   But does one cause the other? If these data were the result of that very unethical experiment we were considering on eighteen-year-olds, then we would conclude that the job had a causal effect on the way the subjects voted. But this table is not the result of an experiment. It is adapted from a survey carried out by Runciman in 1962 and shows the distribution he found already existing among the people he surveyed. There is nothing in the two tables themselves (the results of the experiment and the results of the survey) to tell us which is which. Because this is a survey, we have to be very cautious about concluding that it contains evidence of a causal type to suggest that job causes vote.

6.15   Instead we have to hedge a bit more and say:

If it is reasonable to assume that the type of job is the independent variable and vote is the dependent variable . . . and

if it can be assumed that there is no other variable that we have not controlled which has a systematic effect on both the type of job you do and the way you vote ...

then and only then can we conclude that the job you do has an effect on the way you vote.

6.16 Can we make these two assumptions here? The first one seems reasonable enough. It is unlikely that the way you vote affects the type of job you do. But the second one is much more questionable.

Make a note of other variables that might be operating to invalidate the second assumption.

Fathers job / vote
Own educatio
Age
Sex
Nationality

6.17 I can think of many variables that I would expect to have an effect on both the kind of job you do and the way you vote; your sex, the part of the country you were brought up in, your age, the kind of schooling you have and so on. So the second assumption here cannot really be met; unlike the experimental situation, the non-manual and manual groups were not alike in all other respects. We would have to look at the joint distribution of job and vote with each of the related variables, to be sure that they were not in fact giving rise to the observed association.

6.18 Even though we are not dealing with a strong version of the word 'cause', nonetheless, this table of job type by vote does not enable us to conclude that job causes vote. If we say that the type of job you do has a causal effect on the way you vote, we mean that you could change the way someone voted by making him change jobs. But if I was right in my suspicion that it was not your job that affected your vote directly, but a host of background characteristics that affected both, then making somebody change jobs without changing these background characteristics would have no effect.

6.19 Every time we want to use survey data (i.e. data that was not obtained from an experiment of any sort) to provide evidence of a causal link between two variables, we have to be able to meet the two assumptions mentioned above.

Activity 6
Suppose you carried out a survey and obtained the following information about the age of your respondents and the way in which they voted (Table 23).

Table 23   Hypothetical cross-tabulation of vote by age

	Labour	Conservative	Total
Old	30	21	51
Young	90	30	120
Total	120	51	171

Missing cases	32
Total sample size	203

(a)   Construct a percentage table of the above raw figures and justify your choice of row percentages or column percentages.

(b)   Do the results that you obtained in (a) enable you to draw the conclusion that age has a causal effect on the way you will vote?

7   Single Figure Summaries of Information in a Table

7.1   We have already travelled a long way down the road of reducing the data to the point where it can be made to tell a clear and interesting story. We have reduced the number of rows and columns to the minimum necessary for our purposes, and we have introduced comparability into these rows of columns through using the percentage. But people who spend their time working with data often want to go even further and summarize in a single figure the amount of association they find between two variables in a table.

7.2   As you saw in Block 2, Part 4, when you have two variables that have been measured on an interval scale, a common measure of association to calculate between the two variables is the *product moment correlation coefficient*.

product moment correlation coefficient

What would be the advantage of using the product moment correlation coefficient to summarize the joint distribution of two interval scales, rather than presenting the information in a table? Make a note of your answer and then read on.

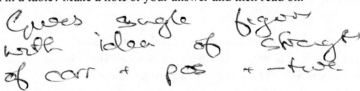

7.3   The information could instead have been grouped into smaller categories and presented in tabular form, but information is lost when the measures are grouped in this way. The correlation coefficient allows you to use the measures you have of each variable (even if each is different) and come up with *one summary* of the extent to which they move together. The correlation coefficient can be positive or negative, and ranges from 0 when there is no correlation at all between two variables to −1 or 1 when there is complete association.

7.4   So when we come to the point of wanting a single measure of association for two nominal scales, the joint distribution of which has been represented in a table, we shall demand the same thing. We want a measure that can be positive or negative, and which ranges from 0 when there is no association to   1 or 1 when the two variables are completely associated. Well, we have already had one in our trusty percentage difference.

(You may want to refresh your mind at this point of the discussion in Block 2, Part 4 about what measures of association are appropriate to different kinds of measurement.)

7.5   All we have to do is work with proportions instead of percentages. You will find that we have a measure of association that meets these criteria for a 2 by 2 table. Look again at Table 10 in which we compared those who had received the pictorial text with those who had not with respect to their pass rates; we found a

Refer back to Table 10

percentage difference of 36.2 which could as easily have been expressed as a proportional difference of 0.362. We could express this either as a positive relationship of +0.362 between 'Having the pictorial version' and 'passing the exam', or as a negative relationship between 'Having the pictorial version' and 'failing the exam'.

7.6 In every 2 by 2 table we have looked at, the positive difference and negative difference were the same figure. You should convince yourself that this will always be a feature of 2 by 2 tables. It is a waste of time to report both figures so we need a rule to tell us which to present.

> *Call one of the categories of each variable the positive category and the other the negative category. Subtract the negative category percentage from the positive category percentage in the positive category of the dependent variable.*

7.7 We shall call this measure of association '*d*' from now on. We shall always refer to it in proportional terms, so that it ranges between 0 and −1 or +1.[4]

d-statistic

7.8 However, percentages and proportions have their limitations. Looking back to Table 14 in which we collapsed the information about social mobility into a 2 by 2 table, we can see that we obtained one single figure: *d* of 0.341 when non-manual was the positive category. But now look back at Table 22 which was a 5 by 2 table. Here we obtained five different figures. And looking at Table 7 we can see that it was not possible in this 7 by 7 table to get directly any *d*'s at all. So we conclude from this that:

Refer back to Table 14

Refer back to Tables 22 and 7

(a) In a 2 by 2 table, *d* summarizes the information contained in a single figure; it acts as a single measure of association.

(b) In a 2 by *c* table (where *c* can be any number of columns) you will obtain *c* different *d*'s.

(c) In an *r* by *c* table (where *r* can be any number of rows) you cannot obtain unambiguous *d*'s without collapsing the table.

7.9 As we saw in section 5 on collapsing tables, different collapses of a *r* by *c* table give you different *d*'s. If the *d*'s obtained from different collapses are very different, you should report the fact and work out what is going on. This is not so much a criticism of *d*, as a reminder that it is not always possible to find one unique figure to summarize the information in a table without a large loss of information.

7.10 It is very important to go to the figures in the most expanded version of the table to check what is going on if you feel at all uneasy about the *d*'s you are getting. The fact that you arrive at different *d*'s illustrates the importance of going back to the figures. This is like the regression analyst who will always check his model by plotting the residuals of *x* and *y* on to the line[5] to see that the information in a particular regression equation is not hiding some important information, like a curve rather than a straight line. Similarly a researcher analysing tables can keep a keen eye on his data by calculating all the different *d*'s obtainable in an *r* by *c* table, just to see if there are any large and dramatic differences.

7.11 But rather than calculate many different *d*'s in an *r* by *c* table, some researchers prefer a measure of association that can be calculated on any table,

---

[4] *It is actually the same thing as the unstandardized regression slope between two dichotomized variables, the values of which are coded 0 and 1, i.e. dummy variables, which will be discussed in Block 7, Part 2. The standardized slope would be 'φ': the square root of the product of forward and backward d.*

[5] *Discussed in Block 7, Part 1 and by D. M. Smith (1975) 'National wealth and infant mortality', reprinted in the Research in Action Reader.*

whatever the numbers of rows and columns, and one which will always produce the same results. We shall not go into the technicalities of any of these here: there are far too many of them and each has its own ardent fans. A common feature of many of them is that they measure association by measuring improved 'predictability': instead of calculating the differences between the proportion of men and the proportion of women who are highly satisfied, as we did in the previous example, such measures would tell you how much better able you would be to predict how satisfied any member of the population was if you first knew whether they were male or female. A correlation coefficient can be interpreted in this way as you can see. (This was discussed in Block 3, Part 1, paragraph 2.14 when considering *proportional-reduction-in-error* as a criterion for measures of association. You may like to look back at the discussion.) If you are interested in following up this discussion see Chapter 7, 'Measures of association for nominal, ordinal and interval variables', Leother and McTavish (1974).

P-R-E

7.12   Not only will you get different *d*'s from different collapses, you will get different *d*'s from percentaging the table the other way round. When we calculated the percentages in the 2 by 2 table of father's class by respondent's class, we arrived at a figure of 0.341 as the difference in percentages. If we had decided to calculate percentages within the categories of respondent's class, we would have a *d* of 0.256. (Check this for yourself and make sure you obtain the same answer.)

7.13   Statisticians call this property of a measure of association, asymmetry. If you are told that a particular measure of association is *asymmetric,* it means that a decision that one of the variables is the independent variable will make a difference to the figure you calculate as the amount of association in the table. So if you really cannot call one of your variables the dependent and one of them the independent, then you could consider using a measure of association that is *symmetric.* You already know one such measure of association for two nominal scales from the discussion in Block 2, Part 4, paragraphs 8.31–8.37; φ would be appropriate to calculate. It turns out that in 2 by 2 tables, φ is the square root of the product of the two possible *d*'s in the table – first taking differences in row percentages and then differences in column percentages. (Check this for yourself on Table 14 where we already know that the 2 *d*'s are 0.341 and 0.256. You should get $\varphi = 0.295$.)

asymmetric association

symmetric association

7.14   Interpreting any table where the marginals of the dependent variable are not representative of the population from which the sample data are drawn is very difficult, and it happens that *d* is the wrong statistic to calculate.

7.15   Let me illustrate this with an example which shows clearly the dangers of doing this. In the medical field, many people are concerned to isolate factors associated with baby-battering, so that social workers can predict who are going to be the mothers who end up battering their children. But they often draw their conclusions from samples that did not have representative proportions of baby-batterers and non-batterers.

7.16   Many of these studies are designed so that a certain number of known baby-batterers are matched with an equal number of non-batterers. These two groups are then compared on a variety of factors. In such a study, one group of 50 known batterers and one of 50 non-batterers were compared with regard to age when they had their first baby. The results looked like this, Table 24.

7.17   These figures do look highly associated, with a *d* of 0.385. Can we conclude from this that if social workers know that a woman had her first baby under the age of twenty that it is best to be suspicious of her as a potential batterer?

Table 24   Cross-tabulation of baby-battering by mother's age at birth of first child

| | Mother's age at birth of first child | | | | d (below 20/20+) |
	Below 20 (prop.)		20 or above (prop.)		
Batterers	25	(0.758)	25	(0.373)	+ 0.385
Non-batterers	8	(0.242)	42	(0.627)	− 0.385
	N=33		N=67		

Source: Hypothetical data but modelled on articles such as Lynch and Roberts (1977)

Think about this for a couple of minutes and make notes on the conclusions you would draw from Table 24.

7.18   We certainly cannot make predictions like that on the basis of this table. The reason why is because the population as a whole is not made up of 50 per cent baby-batterers. The known population percentage is more like 0.2 per cent. Imagine what a table would look like if the same shape of relationship were kept between mother's age at birth of first child and battering, but the marginals were manipulated to make them like the general population marginals: I have made it 20:10 000 instead of 20:9 980 for ease (Table 25).

Table 25   Reworking Table 23 with representative marginals

| | Mother's age at birth of first child | | | | d (below 20/20+) |
	Below 20 (prop.)		20 or above (prop.)		
Batterers	10	(0.006)	10	(0.001)	+ 0.005
Non-batterers	600	(0.994)	8 400	(0.999)	− 0.005
	N=610		N=8 410		

7.19   We get a more realistic d of 0.005. So do be very careful every time you inspect a table where the marginals on the variable that you are trying to explain are not representative of the population as a whole. Finally, a rule which you would do well to learn:

Never calculate d's when your marginals on the dependent variable are not representative of the population as a whole.

7.20   *The statistic d, summary*   We have chosen to use d throughout this Part because we think it has great virtues:

(a)   It is simple to calculate.

(b)   It ranges between 0 when there is no association to + 1 or − 1 when there is complete association.

(c)   Even the non-statistical layman can make sense of d without much difficulty.

(d)   It has an approximately normal sampling distribution (as you will discover in the next section).

But there are three points that you must always bear in mind when you use d:

(a)   Different collapses will give you different d's.

(b)   Reversing the direction of the relationships, i.e. reversing the dependent and independent variable, will give you different d's.

(c)   When the marginals on the dependent variable are not representative, d is not the appropriate statistic to calculate.

8   Generalizing Beyond Your Data

8.1   Paradoxically, we are not usually interested in the people whom we are studying. We select a *sample* of people to study, not because of any intrinsically interesting properties that *they* may have, but because we hope that they will tell us something about the general population from which they are drawn. (Block 3, Part 4, section 2 deals with the purpose of sampling from populations.)

sample

8.2   We need only pick a sample because *so long as the sample is selected at random,* we know that it reflects more or less accurately the characteristics of the population from which it was drawn. (Historical note: This is quite a recent development in research techniques and one that has not always been accepted. There still lingers on in social research a hankering after samples which are purposively drawn so as to be representative, or so as to match another group. You should refer to Block 3, Part 4 to remind yourself why random samples are better.)

8.3   But now we have got to face the fact that, when we are dealing with sample data, there is always the possibility that the particular sample that we happened to draw was a fluke in some way or another. It might be that we happened to draw a set of individuals who did not show a relationship between age and vote when in fact there was such an association in the population from which they were drawn. Or we might have come across an association between age and vote in our sample when there was no such association in the population. We have got to devise a way of deciding what the likelihood is that our particular sample result was indeed the result of such a fluke.

8.4   Social scientists have traditionally approached this problem in two rather different ways. One group have argued that the way to generalize from your sample result to the population is to calculate an interval into which the measure of association is likely to fall. Instead of saying that the difference in percentages between age and vote is 53 per cent, they calculate what is the lowest likely amount of association and what is the highest amount of association, so that instead of saying that d is 0.53, they prefer to make a probability statement like 'd is 0.53 give or take 0.06'. The other group have argued that the really important question to ask is whether it is possible that the two variables under consideration could be independent of one another in the population from which the sample was drawn; they argue that the size of a particular sample d is relatively uninteresting compared with the question: 'Is it 0 or not?'. This group end up *making a decision.* Such people test the hypothesis that a given d found in a sample comes, in all probability, from a population in which there is no association between two variables. The next **Part of Block 6** *Hypothesis Testing* treats this problem and the techniques needed to deal with it. We shall conclude this Part by answering the question: 'Given a value of d based on sample data, what is the likely range of values for d in the population from which the sample comes?'.

Constructing a Confidence Interval for *d*

8.5   When we are dealing with sample data, the actual figure we get for the measure of association between two variables is only an *estimate* when applied to the population as a whole. It is the best estimate that we can make but it is still only a calculation of what we think the true population value *might be*. Let us use as an example, Table 18, the first of the two tables that we constructed to examine the amount of association between sex and satisfaction with one's district. We calculated a *d* in the first instance of 0.370. If a town planner had asked you for the best guess you could make of the true value for D[6] in the population from which this sample was drawn (i.e. the adult population resident in the urban areas of the UK) you would say 0.370 if you had to estimate one single figure. Or you could have been more precise and calculated it correct to more decimal places and arrived at a single estimate of *d* of 0.3705. This would then have been your best guess of the real population value of *D*, the real difference between men and women with respect to satisfaction levels considered in the population from whom the sample was drawn.

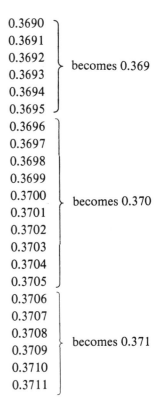

8.6   Why did I not report it as 0.3705? Here is another paradox: although 0.3705 is indeed our best single estimate of what the population *D* is, it is extremely unlikely to be spot-on accurate, so I decided that it was not worth giving the illusion of accuracy by presenting four decimal places. No single figure is going to be accurate and the more decimal places we report, the less likely it is to be accurate. It would be much better if we could report a range of values in which the population *D* is likely to fall.

8.7   Suppose you convinced the town planner of this and he then asked you to make the best estimate you could of the *range* of values the population *D* would be in. Well, if you think about it, you did already imply a range when you gave him the point estimate of 0.370 saying that our estimate of the population *D* was 0.370 rounded to three decimal places, was equivalent to saying that the *D* was somewhere between 0.3696 and 0.3705 (following a conventional rounding rule).

8.8   But when the decision was made to round to three decimal places, it was somewhat arbitrary; we had not done calculations which told us that the most probable range for *D* to be in was between 0.3696 and 0.3705. Now we want to do just that; we want to calculate an *interval estimate* which will tell us in what range of figures we may reasonably expect to find *D*. We want to know, in other words, not only that the best *point estimate* is 0.370 but whether it could be as low as 0.170 and as high as 0.570 or whether it is really quite a tight estimate, which is unlikely to be below 0.350 or above 0.390. So, instead of conveying a false sense of accuracy, when asked by the town planner to make an interval estimate of what *D* was in the population, you should have said: 'How accurate do you want my method of estimation to be? I can either use a very accurate method which will yield a wide range of values, or not such an accurate method which will yield a narrower range of values'. Let us suppose he replied: 'Use a method which is accurate 95 per cent of the time'.

8.9   In order to calculate this, we make use of the sampling distribution of *d*. Even suppose we knew from some other source – for instance the Census – that the true population *D* was 0.370, we would still expect that if we drew large numbers of samples of 143 men and 84 women from the population they would all be slightly different, owing to chance fluctuations from the particular samples we happened to draw. Now for the good news: the sampling distribution obtained from drawing repeated samples of a particular size and calculating *d* on each is approximately normal (Block 3, Part 4).

interval estimate

point estimate

---

[6] *We shall use the convention of calling the sample value* d *and the population value* D.

Make short notes on why you think I call this good news. What can we say the minute we know that a distribution is normal?

[handwritten: Can yours use means / variance / SD]

8.10 We should be pleased that the sampling distribution is *normal* because of the simplicity of the normal curve; even though the precise mathematical formula which defines the curve is rather complex, all we need to know about any normal curve is the mean and standard deviation of the distribution, and then we can draw it exactly. More importantly, in any *normal distribution*, 95 per cent of the cases lie approximately two standard deviation units to either side of the mean of the distribution. (If you are finding this difficult to follow, go back to the beginning of this section on generalizing beyond your data and read through it again slowly. If you reach this point once again and are feeling very lost do the following activity, and if that does not help, go back to Block 3, Part 4 to revise the concepts from sampling.)

normal distribution

Activity 7

You probably have got in your house at this moment a kit which will enable you to try out for yourself what happens to sample statistics when you calculate them on repeated random samples from a population with a known characteristic. All you need is a pack of cards.

We shall calculate the difference in proportions, d, between the red cards and the black cards in the pack with respect to the number of face cards – Jacks, Queens and Kings, each contains. In one pack of cards we know that the true d is 0, since p_1 is 6/26 and p_2 is also 6/26. Now try for yourself and see what different values of d you get when you sample ten blacks and ten reds, and calculate the difference in the proportion of face cards you find.

(a)   Remove the Jokers if there are any and split the pack into a black pile and a red pile.

(b)   Starting with the red pile, cut it ten times, shuffling after each cut and note down how many times you turn up a face card.

(c)   Do the same with the black pile.

(d)   Calculate the d and write it down, noting whether it was positive (when red is more than black) or negative (black more than red).

(e)   Repeat b, c and d, ten times.

(f)   Make a histogram of the results and compare this with the normal distribution.

8.11 Are you beginning to see how we are going to use the simplicity of the normal distribution to do the job we discussed: to construct an interval estimate for the population d when all we know is that the d between two samples of 143 and 84 is 0.370? The minute we know that standard deviation of the sampling distribution of d (we usually call this 'the standard error of d') we can use the information about the areas under the normal curve to calculate where 95 per cent of all results of repeated random sampling will fall. Our best estimate for d is 0.370. Now we also know that 95 per cent of all the d's calculated on random samples of 143 men and 84 women will fall 2 standard deviations (σ) to either side

See Block 3, Part 4

of this. If we calculate and present an interval estimate for d which ranges 2 σ either side of the best estimate, by definition we are using a method which will contain the true proportion d 95 times in 100. What did the town planner ask us to do? Precisely that! All we have to do is find out the value of σ and we shall have solved our problem.

8.12   Let us review at this stage what we do and do not know.

We know:

(a)   The sample d (0.370) which we obtained by subtracting the proportion, high satisfaction with district among men (p_1) from the proportion, high satisfaction with district among women (p_2).

(b)   The sample number (n_1) of men (143) and the sample number (n_2) of women (84).

But we do not know:

(a)   The true population D (following the convention of calling the population parameters by capital letters) between P_1 and P_2.

(b)   The mean of the sampling distribution of D.

(c)   The standard error of the sampling distribution of D.

8.13   Now let us fill those gaps. We have already decided that the sample d is the best estimate we can make of the true population D. So let us assume that we know that the population D is 0.370. Now we ask: 'What is the shape of the distribution of d's that we would get if we drew large numbers of samples of 143 men and 84 women at random and calculated the d between p_1 and p_2, when the true population D was fixed at 0.370?'.

8.14   Well, mathematicians assure us that:

(a)   the resulting sampling distribution is normal,

(b)   with a mean equal to the true population D (here 0.370) and

(c)   a standard error of:

$$\sqrt{\frac{p_1(1-p_1)}{n_1} + \frac{p_2(1-p_2)}{n_2}}$$

Here again, we do not know the true population proportions P_1 and P_2, but we shall substitute the sample p's. Notice that when the proportions are 0.30/0.70 or less skewed, $(p)(1-p)$ only varies between 0.21 and 0.25, so some people prefer to be conservative and to use 0.25 in the numerators of the formula for the standard error. Note that, mathematically, the numerators will be at a maximum when $p_1 = (1-p_1) = 0.5$, so that $p_1(1-p_1) = 0.25$.

8.15   Calculating this is quite straightforward with the help of a calculator; watch out for the decimal points, for we shall be dealing with figures that have a lot of zeros.

$$\sqrt{\frac{(0.93)(0.07)}{143} + \frac{(0.56)(0.44)}{84}}$$
$$= \sqrt{0.000455 + 0.002933}$$
$$= \sqrt{0.003388}$$
$$= 0.058$$

8.16   All we have left to do is to define 'probable' as something which might be expected to happen 95 per cent of the time. We can say that the true population value of d is probably 0.370 give or take 2×0.058, i.e. somewhere between 0.254 and 0.486. Or we could express this in a rather more mathematical-looking form and say $d = 0.370 \pm 0.116$, p (for probability) $= 0.95$. Or we could say that we constructed a 95 per cent confidence interval for d which was $0.254 - 0.486$.

Figure 7   Sampling distribution of d with $n_1 = 143$ and $n_2 = 84$, $D = 0.370$ and $s_d = 0.058$

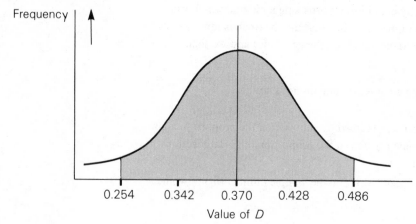

8.17   So we were giving the impression of too much accuracy when we said that the best estimate of the population parameter was 0.370; that was the best point estimate, but the best interval estimate for it ranges from 0.254 to 0.486 (at $p = 0.95$) which is nothing like so precise.

Activity 8

We have just constructed an interval estimate for the d we calculated in Table 18, the first version of the table dichotomized to show the relationship between sex and satisfaction with district. Calculate an interval estimate for d in Table 19. This should take you about fifteen minutes.

---

9   Conclusion

9.1   The best way to familiarize yourself with these ideas is to try them out. There is an activity which follows with a summary, Appendix 1, to help you remember what you have learnt so far. When you have done it, try taking a table you have read in a newspaper or in a social science book, and apply these ideas to it.

9.2   Do not skip over tables in a text when you read it. It is hard work, as you now realize, but if you conscientiously try to read every table that you meet in a text, you will find it gets easier and easier. You did not learn to read letters overnight. Reading numbers will not take so long if you give it a chance!

Activity 9

The 1976 US General Social Survey also has data on the respondents' self-placement in terms of social class; 'If you were asked to use one of four names for your social class, which would you say you belonged in: the lower class, the working class, the middle class or the upper class?'. The variable is dichotomized as:

High = middle class, upper class
Low = working class, lower class

I was interested in the relationship between father's education and respondent's class placement. So I asked the computer to run their cross-tabulation. Unfortunately the results were a bit garbled. What I learned was this:

303 cases scored high on both items
$N = 1082$
Total sample size $= 1499$
547 cases were scored high on class
219 cases were scored high on father's education and low on respondent's class
Two sigma confidence interval for $d = \pm 0.06$

(a)   Use these figures to fill in the complete four-fold table, as in Table 13.

(b)   Find the marginal proportions for respondent's class.

(c)   Decide which is the independent variable and which is the dependent variable. Justify your decision briefly.

(d)   Calculate d.

(e)   Translate the numerical results into a brief sentence or two.

Objectives

After studying Block 6, Part 2, you should be able to:

1   Differentiate between tables designed as a 'storehouse' of information and those designed to provide an immediate impression of trends.

2   Distinguish marginal distributions from joint distributions.

3   Define the following terms:
Case, table, column, row, total, marginal, cell, cell frequency, cross-tabulation, joint distribution, asymmetry.

4   Allocate cases to the cells in a table, add the resultant column and row cell frequencies and derive marginals and totals.

5   Describe the advantages and limitations of tabular data and graphical displays.

6   Convert the cell frequencies in a given table into percentages and describe the advantages these provide for subsequent data analysis.

7   Interpret row and column percentages.

8   Describe the advantages and disadvantages of collapsing data in a table.

9   Identify redundant material in a given table and reduce the table to an efficient form.

10   Describe and illustrate how the level of measurement associated with given data can influence any decision to collapse it into a new form.

11   Describe and illustrate how different collapses of data in a table may lead to different interpretations.

12   Describe the difficulties of inferring causal relationships from data derived from tables.

13   Evaluate a given hypothesis from data represented in tabular form.

14   Summarize, in a single figure (d) the amount of association between two variables in a table.

15   Describe how the number of rows and columns in a table influence the number of d's, or even the ability to derive them.

16   Describe, in the context of a 2 by 2 table, the property of asymmetry on a calculated d.

17   Describe the characteristics of the index d.

18   Describe and illustrate how different collapses of a table will give different d's.

19 Describe and illustrate how reversing the direction of the relationship (i.e. reversing the dependent/independent variables) will give different d's.

20 Describe and illustrate the importance of only calculating d's when the marginals on the dependent variable are representative of the population as a whole.

21 Distinguish the point estimate of a d from a confidence interval for d.

Appendix 1: Working Through a Table

The following is a set of procedures which should help you to develop a routine both for constructing tables of your own and reading those of others. Notice that I have not always followed them myself in the text where I wished to emphasize that the main point was clarity and many of the examples were hypothesized. In a research paper, the following are essential.

Making Your Own Table	Reading Other People's
Give each table a unique identifier, perhaps consistent with chapter numbers.	
Give a short, understandable, accurate title.	Read the title.
Report the questions asked, the population sampled and the source and the date of the data.	Look to see the exact question asked, the population sampled and the source and the date of the data. Are they the results of an experiment or a survey?
Collapse the table to the minimum number of rows and columns necessary; if you are going to calculate d, as we have shown you in this Part, make each table into a 2 by 2. But save the original tables in case other researchers want to use them.	Do not collapse someone else's table before you have read it all through. Go back to the original raw cell frequencies to collapse someone else's data.
Label each of the variables carefully, not just as x and y.	Read the variable labels.
Label each of the categories carefully.	Read the category labels.
Use white space and grid lines to set the table out clearly.	
You might decide to order the rows and columns to reflect their relative sizes, i.e. so that they run in decreasing order. But there might be a conventional order for them.	See if there is any logic in the ordering of the rows and columns.

Making Your Own Table	**Reading Other People's**
Exclude missing data from the table, but report how many cases are excluded. Distinguish between those people who found the question *inapplicable* from those who did not reply. It would be good practice not only to report the number who did not answer individual questions but also the number who did not respond to the original request for interview.	Note how many people did not or could not reply to the questions. Add this number to the original number of non-respondents to get a real picture of response rate to the question. This information should give you very important clues about the interpretation of the question.
Decide which variable will label the rows and which the columns by a combination of the following three rules which may be in conflict: (a) It is easier to compare figures which are physically close to each other. (b) It is easier to compare figures down a column than across a row. (c) If columns are used for figures that vary little then the regularity and deviations from regularity will be more easy to spot. But get used to a pattern and stick to it. Hereafter, I shall give you one set of rules which I find useful.	

Raw Data

Put the raw cell frequencies into the cells. Check everything adds up correctly.	
Check that there are no exceptional cases which should be excluded.	
Decide how much raw data to present and how much can be put in an appendix. The more fully you document in an appendix, the more artistic you can be in your text, for you will not need to clutter the page.	
Decide whether raw data will be sufficient. Usually you will want to construct percentage tables.	If no percentages have been calculated for you, you cross the middle line and carry on from here as if you were constructing your own table.

←

Percentage Tables

Use a fixed rounding convention, e.g. rounding to an even number.	
Distinguish between a real 0 (i.e. no cases) and rounding down to 0.	Check how real 0 and rounding down to 0 are distinguished.
Decide how many decimal places you will round to. If you have no idea, start rounding to 3 decimal places with proportions, 1 with percentages.	Check how many decimal places the data exhibit.

Making Your Own Table	Reading Other People's
Make sure throughout that there can be no confusion between real numbers and percentages/proportions. Label every column 'per cent' or 'proportion'; perhaps even place per cent after the first number in each row.	Look to see which are the real numbers and which the percentages/proportions. Disregard the real numbers and concentrate on the percentages/proportions from now on.
Decide which is the dependent variable; make the categories of the independent variable add up to 100, i.e. percentage within categories of the independent variable.	Decide which is the dependent variable. Look at the marginal frequencies and check that they are roughly representative of the population from which they were drawn.
Always point out and explain when numbers do not add up to 100 because of rounding. Never present percentages that are not to be summed as if they should be, i.e. by placing them close together in a column. If this is unavoidable, point out to a reader that they do not add up to 100 per cent.	Look to see which way the percentages/proportions have been presented. If this is not immediately clear, check by adding up the numbers in the first row and column to see which way you get 100. If you do not get 100 either way, the percentages are probably meant to run with their 'shadow', i.e. 23 per cent who did . . . implying 77 per cent who did not.
Always report the minimum number of N's for the entire frequency table to be reconstructed.	If you do not like the way the percentages/proportions have been presented, reconstruct the frequency table and recalculate them.
Place N's in brackets and set them clearly apart from the percentages/proportions.	
Do not calculate percentages when N is less than 20 cases. Put in asterisk instead and explain in a footnote.	Check that none of the percentages have been calculated on less than 20 cases, i.e. calling five, 20 per cent of 25 is O.K. But calling two, 20 per cent of 10 is not.

With R by C Tables

	Start by looking at the percentage in the first margin of the dependent variable. This is what you would 'expect' to find in each category of the independent variable if there was no association between the independent and the dependent variable.
	Compare this percentage with the percentage you had in each category of the independent variable. Make a note of the discrepancy between this and the figure you 'expected'.
	Then go to the next marginal percentage in the dependent variable and repeat the process. Do this until you have examined every figure in the table.

With 2 by 2 Tables Calculate *d*

(a) (i) Decide which is to be the positive and which the negative category with each of your variables.

(ii) Check that the marginals on the dependent variables are representative of the population.

(b) Go to the positive category of the dependent variable. Subtract the negative category percentage from the positive category percentage.

(c) The result is *d*, and will be either positive or negative. If the result is negative, you should consider renaming the categories of the independent variable, reversing positive and negative, so that your resulting *d* will be positive.

(d) If you were working from a collapsed table, check that if you had collapsed it another way you would have got a similar estimate of *d*. If you do not, work out what is going on.

To Calculate 95 per cent Confidence Intervals for *d*

(a) Use sample *d* as best estimate of the true population *D*.

(b) Calculate s_d using this formula:

$$\sqrt{\frac{p_1(1-p_1)}{n_1} + \frac{p_2(1-p_2)}{n_2}}$$

(Remember: You calculated *d* by subtracting p_2 from p_1. n_1 is the marginal for the positive category of the independent variable and n_2 is the marginal for the negative category.)

(c) Write down the result like this:

$$D = (\text{sampled } d) \pm \times 2 s_d$$

Deciding What the Results Mean

Decide if you can conclude that there is a relationship between these two variables or not, noting:
How strong it is.
What sign it has.

Is this evidence of a causal effect of the independent variable on the dependent variable? How is that causal effect operating? Or might it be that there is a third variable affecting both and explaining this relationship? What could that be?

If these are experimental data, you may conclude that the independent variable is having some causal effect on the dependent variable.

If these are survey data, you must say:
If it is reasonable to assume that *x* is the independent variable and *y* is the dependent variable; and
if it can be assumed that there is no other variable which has a systematic effect on both *x* and *y*;
then we may conclude that *x* causes *y*.

Appendix 2: Introducing a Third Variable

Prepared by David Fruin for the Course Team

1 Introduction

1.1 Block 6, Part 2 introduced you to certain techniques for constructing and analysing 2 by 2 tables where variables are basically dichotomous – male/female, employed/unemployed, state school/private school – or where categories of the variable can be grouped together to construct a dichotomy – social class, number of children, age, academic performance. Since most data in tables can be collapsed into 2 by 2 tables, such techniques are important and are widely used by educational and social researchers. These techniques are particularly suitable for hand calculation and we expect you to use them when analysing your own Survey Project data.

1.2 However it is rare that a single 2 by 2 table can adequately summarize a real-world situation or process in which researchers are interested. Hypotheses about real life and the tables which represent them usually need the qualification 'other things being equal'. All too frequently other things *are not* equal and we need to take into account other important variables. When researchers do this systematically and statistically they are carrying out *multivariate analysis*. You might encounter multivariate analysis in a more complex form in Part 2 of Block 7 where you are introduced to the General Linear Model[1].

1.3 The purpose of this Appendix is to show you a few simple techniques which extend the sort of analysis which Cathie Marsh has introduced and which you should consider using on your own Survey Project material in order to explore your data more fully. The techniques used here need only the *d*-statistic which should now be familiar to you and is easy to calculate. The calculations will therefore be relatively straightforward although the ideas of Part 2 will be extended.

1.4 The aims of this Appendix are to enable you to:
(a) Say what is meant by a test factor.

(b) Construct 2 by 2 partial association tables for two dichotomized variables and a test factor.

(c) Calculate partial *d*-statistics.

(d) Recognize statistical interaction in partial association tables and interpret it.

(e) Recognize cases of spurious association and suppressed association and interpret them.

2 Introducing a Third Variable

2.1 In Part 2 (pp. 48–9) of this Block you examined some 2 by 2 tables and a three-dimensional histogram based on data from the Oxford Mobility Project. In this Appendix we shall use some similar but imaginary data to explore the effect of introducing a third variable into our analysis and in Table 1 we present cross-tabulated data on social class and political party identity for 100 respondents.

---

[1]*Parts 2 and 3 of Block 7 are optional course material; you will not be examined on them.*

Table 1   Social class and political party identity for 100 imaginary respondents
(Cell entries are frequencies)

| | | Social class | | | | |
		Highest 1	2	3	4	Lowest 5
Political party identity	Conservative	12	12	8	6	8
	Labour	5	5	7	9	6
	Liberal	2	2	5	2	2
	Other	1	1	2	4	1

2.2   Let us assume that we wish to test the hypothesis that higher social class is
associated with increased conservatism, measured for the present purpose by
political party identity. This suggests fairly directly that we should collapse the
party identity variable into two categories, Conservative and All others. (If we had
been investigating the converse hypothesis that people of lower social class were
more radical than people of higher social class, we would probably use the
categories of Labour and All other.) In the absence of a theoretical basis for
splitting the social class variable, the 'best' division, in terms of most closely
approximating a 50:50 split, is to combine the first two categories into a 'higher'
group and the last three categories into a 'lower' group. The joint distribution for
these collapsed variables is shown in Table 2.

Table 2   Collapsed version of Table 1 *(Cell entries are frequencies)*

| | | Social class | |
		Higher 1 and 2	Lower 3, 4 and 5
Political party identity	Conservative	24	20
	All other	16	40
	Total	40	60

2.3   For our research hypothesis, the main interest lies in examining the effect
which social class has upon party identity and not the effect which party identity
has on social class, although we could hypothesize a series of causal links which
might suggest that people with particular political views and attitudes tend to seek
and to avoid certain types of employment which determine social class allocation.
But in the present context, we are hypothesizing that party identity is dependent
on social class, i.e. party identity is the dependent variable and social class is the
independent variable. This causal relationship has been illustrated in the same
fashion as we portrayed, on page 55 of Block 6, Part 2, the effect which different
teaching methods have on success at statistics.

Figure 1

We will investigate this hypothesis by examining the association between these
two variable using the d-statistic following the rules which Cathie Marsh spelled
out. We first need to express the raw frequencies as proportions calculated within

the categories of the independent variable (social class). Since we expect that the Conservative category and the higher social class group will go together, we can regard these two as the positive categories. Table 3 presents these proportions.

Table 3   Social class and political party identity: calculating *d* *(Cell entries are proportions)*

			Social class (Independent variable)		
			High (+)	Low (−)	*d*
Political party identity	(Dependent variable)	Conservative (+) All other (−)	.600 .400	.333 .667	+.267
		Total	1.000	1.000	

2.4   In the usual way, we calculate *d* by locating the positive row of the dependent variable (Conservative) and then substracting the negative category proportion of the independent variable from the positive category of the same variable, i.e. in our case we subtract .333 from .600 to obtain +.267 (the plus sign is important) to obtain the *d* value required. This suggests that there is, as we hypothesized, a slight positive (because of the plus sign) association between being in the higher social class and identifying with the Conservative Party. We need however to take into account the standard error of *d*, s_d, which we calculate using the formula on page 75 of Block 6:

$$s_d = \frac{.600 \times .400}{40} + \frac{.333 \times .667}{60}$$
$$= .093$$

Thus the 95% confidence interval for our value of +.267 is .267 ± (2 × .093), i.e. from +.081 to +.453. Although a fairly wide range, these values suggest that the true *d* is very likely to be positive.

2.5   With such a complex topic as political party identity to look only at a single variable explanation must inevitably be regarded as incomplete. More complex analyses need to take into account at least, say, age as a determinant implying a model such as that in Figure 2.

Figure 2

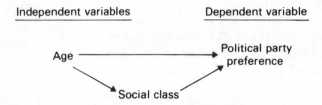

The causal model of this diagram keeps social class as a determining factor but introduces age as a determining factor, both of party political preferences and of social class. We can take age into account by using the technique of *partial association*. (The general term for this technique is partial correlation but with dichotomized variables the more correct term is 'association'.) The partial association procedure consists of examining the association, measured in terms of *d*, when we control for age. Controlling for age means attempting to eliminate its effect by dividing the overall sample into two subsamples each of which contains groups of similarly aged people.

2.6 The general procedures for calculating partial association tables for dichotomized variables are as follows:

1 You will need access to a listing or original three-way raw data tables which can provide information for individuals or groups about their values with respect to each of the three (dichotomized) variables being studied.

2 Divide the total sample into two groups according to the two categories of the control variable, in our example this will be *age*.

3 For the two levels of the control variable, cross-tabulate the two sub-groups for the two other variables in the usual way, obtaining from the raw numbers the proportions needed to calculate *d*.

4 Calculate the *partial d*s for the 2 by 2 tables and compare these two values with each other and with the *d* for the total sample.

Where data are stored in computers, it is often possible to request that the partial association tables be printed directly without going back to the basic data.

When we introduce a third variable into our analysis, in the present example, age, we can consider it as a *test factor* since we used it to test the relationship found in the single (combined) 2 by 2 table to see if it holds when the test factor is brought into the picture.

2.7 In our case we will assume that we have access to the necessary basic data and that we dichotomize the age variable to obtain one group categorized as younger, say people aged 20 to 39, and another group categorized as older, say 40 to 59. For our imaginary data we might obtain the pair of cross-tabulations shown in Table 4 which presents both the cell frequencies and the appropriate proportions.

Table 4 Partial association between social class and political party, controlling for age: calculating *d*s
(Cell entries are numbers (n) and proportions (p))

| *Young (20–39)* | | Social class | | | | |
| | | High | | Low | | |
		n	*p*	*n*	*p*	*d*
Political party identity	Conservative	9	.474	9	.281	.193
	All others	10	.526	23	.719	
	Total	19	1.000	32	1.000	

| *Old (40–59)* | | Social class | | | | |
| | | High | | Low | | |
		n	*p*	*n*	*p*	*d*
Political party identity	Conservative	15	.714	11	.393	.321
	All others	6	.286	17	.607	
	Total	21	1.000	28	1.000	

The partial association *d*s for the two sub-groups are shown to be +.193 for the younger group and +.321 for the older group. How should we interpret these two figures? The low *d* value .193 (whose 95% confidence interval includes zero) suggests that for younger people social class does not have a strong effect on choice of political party identity. In contrast, the higher value of .321 (whose 95% confidence range is from +.051 to +.591) suggests that older people's political preference is more strongly associated with social class. In real life we would need to treat these figures and the interpretation with caution since the effect might be a cohort effect, limited to particular sets of generation who shared similar experiences. Whether it would apply, for example, to people born since the Second World War would remain to be seen. In addition for a fuller explanatory investigation we would probably wish to include in our multivariate analysis other variables such as sex and income.

3   Differing patterns

3.1   When we use the partial association technique it is usual to find that the two partial ds diverge from the d obtained before controlling for a test factor.

What values would you have expected for the partial association ds if controlling for age had had no effect? Make a brief note and compare your answer to what follows below.

Be same as orig d,

If controlling for age had had no effect on the association between social class and party identity, we would have found that both partial ds would be unchanged from the original value of .267. This was not the case of course and instead results in Table 4 demonstrate a clear *statistical interaction* between age and the association between social class and political party identity. In general, a statistical interaction exists where the relationship between the first two variables is different for one category of the test factor compared to the relationship for the other category.

3.2   Sometimes when we carry out partial association analysis we may reveal strong but contrasting associations in our partial ds even though no association was present for the overall d, calculated before introducing the test factor: such cases are referred to as examples of *suppressed association*. For example, we might imagine an inquiry set up to investigate whether three years of full-time university education changes students' political party preference, gathering data from students at entry to university and on leaving, with results such as those in Table 5.

Table 5   Time at university and political party preference
(Cell entries are proportions)

			(Independent variable)		
			On entry to university (−)	On leaving university (+)	d
Political party preference	(Dependent variable)	Labour (+) All others (−)	.400 .600	.400 .600	0
		Total	1.000	1.000	

The d value of zero indicates an absence of association between the two variables. However, we might suspect that whether students took Arts or Sciences as a main course could have an effect so that we might wish to use type of course taken as a test factor, with the hypothetical results of Table 6.

Table 6   Time at university and political party preference: controlling for type of main course *(Cell entries are proportions)*

		On entry to university (−)	On leaving university (+)	*d*
Art students				
Political party preference	Labour (+)	.400	.500	+.100
	All other (−)	.600	.500	
	Total	1.000	1.000	
Science students				
Political party preference	Labour (+)	.400	.300	−.100
	All other (−)	.600	.700	
	Total	1.000	1.000	

The partial *d*s are +.100 and −.100 for the Arts and Science subject students respectively, suggesting that the three years at university have different effects on different types of students, leading to Arts students increasing their preference for Labour while Science students decrease their preference for Labour. Introducing the test factor of 'type of course taken' has revealed the relationship which was earlier suppressed.

3.3   In contrast, sometimes an overall *d* may indicate an association between a pair of variables but the association disappears when a test factor is introduced. In such cases we refer to the initial apparent association as a *spurious association*. For example, we might be studying the effect of type of school, say comprehensive and grammar, on academic achievement, measured perhaps in 'O' level performance. Table 7 presents hypothetical data and for a change I have swapped round the dependent and independent variables so that the values of the independent variable correspond to rows.

Table 7   Type of school and academic performance *(Cell entries are proportions)*

		Academic achievement (Dependent variable)		
		High (+)	Low (−)	Total
School type (Independent variable)	Grammar (+)	.667	.333	1.000
	Comprehensive (−)	.432	.568	1.000
	d	+.235		

The obtained *d* value of +.235 shows that there is an association between attending grammar school and doing well at 'O' levels. However, if we control for children's ability on entry to the schools, perhaps measured by aptitude tests given at age 11, we might obtain the following partial association tables as shown in Table 8. Both partial *d*s are now zero. The association of Table 7 is revealed as a spurious association attributable to the different mixes of pupils' ability for the two types of school. Grammar schools, in this imaginary example, appear to do better but this is shown to be due to having a higher proportion of the more able pupils.

3.4   In real-life examples, neither spurious associations nor suppressed associations would usually stand out so clearly as in our imaginary data presented

Table 8   Type of school and academic achievement: controlling for ability at entry *(Cell entries are proportions)*

| | | Academic achievement | | |
		High (+)	Low (−)	Total
High entry ability				
School	Grammar (+)	.750	.250	1.000
type	Comprehensive (−)	.750	.250	1.000
	d	0		
Low entry ability				
School	Grammar (+)	.250	.750	1.000
type	Comprehensive (−)	.250	.750	1.000
	d	0		

here. We also need to take into account the likely range of the true population values of d, via the standard error, s_d, something which we did not examine in Tables 6, 7 and 8. We also need to be aware that just as in the 2 by 2 analyses of Block 6, Part 2, where different collapses of multivalued variables were shown to lead to different ds, so too can different partial association ds be obtained from different collapses of the control variable/test factor.

3.5   Three-way partial association techniques can also serve as a basis for extending our analysis to include four or more variables. A re-examination of Figure 2 where there are two pathways from Age to Political party identity (one via the social class variable) should alert us also to the need for additional techniques to be able to assess in quantitative form the contribution which casual variables may have, both directly and indirectly, on some final dependent variable. This is best done by techniques of multiple regression, using three or more independent variables, but this is beyond the scope of the course. Block 7, Parts 2 and 3, show how this is done but their contents are not examinable.

Summary of Steps to Take when Introducing a Third Variable to a Two Variable Analysis

(a)   Keep clearly in mind which is the dependent variable in your initial two variable analysis.

(b)   Draw a simple diagram, as in Figure 1, to show independent and dependent variables.

(c)   Choose one or more test factors. A test factor should be related to the dependent variable on theoretical grounds, i.e. it should be one which *could* account for variation in the dependent variable.

(d)   Re-draw your diagram to indicate how the three variables could be inter-related. Alternative diagrams could represent different possible causal relationships.

(e)   Where different possibilities exist for dichotomizing the test factor you may need to repeat your partial association analysis to examine different theoretical and empirical possibilities for dividing your sample on the test factor.

(f)   Examine your pairs of partial association tables noting the direction and strength of the partial ds, taking into account the likely range for an estimate of the population ds, derived from calculation of the standard errors.

(g)   See if your tables provide evidence of either spurious or suppressed association and consider the effect these have on interpreting your results.

Recommended Reading

ROSENBERG, M. (1968) 'Extraneous variables', reprinted in Bynner, J. and Stribley, K. M. (eds) (1979) *Social research: principles and procedures*, London, Longman/The Open University Press, Ch. 20.

Further Reading

DAVIS, J. A. (1971) *Elementary survey analysis*. London, Prentice-Hall. This book offers a complete scheme for dealing with the analysis of surveys, based on dichotomized variables. It is similar in approach to Cathie Marsh's treatment in Block 6.

Acknowledgements

Much of the structure and ideas of this appendix derive from an earlier version written by Michael Wilson.

Answers to Activities

Activity 1

Compare your result with Table 4 where the complete allocation of all the cases comprising $N (= 8575)$ respondents is 'stored'.

Activity 2

(a)   Find the column headed 'Respondent's class – category 3', and look for the total at the foot of the column. This is 827 cases.

(b)   Now decide what your base is. The question asks you to 'calculate the percentage and the proportion *of the total of respondents* . . . who were in social class 3'. This gives you the base if you read it carefully. The grand total of respondents is $N = 8575$, in the bottom right-hand corner of Table 4.

(c)   Now calculate the proportion as $827/8575 = 0.096$. To find the percentage simply multiply this proportion by 100 to get 9.6 per cent.

Activity 3

Feigehen uses a rather neat way of presenting his percentages. He does not bother with presenting the information about those who were not in poverty, since this is always derivable from the information about those who were. He calls the row percentages, which calculate the percentages within each household size, the 'risk of poverty'. In other words, he uses the information that 20.7 per cent of one-person households are in poverty to say that there is a 20.7 per cent 'risk' of poverty among this group. He calls the column percentages the 'accountability for poverty'; looking at the same group of 259 single household people who were in poverty, we know that they 'accounted for' 50.8 per cent of all those households in poverty. So the results are like this (Table 26).

Table 26

Number in household	Risk of poverty	Accountability for poverty	N
1	20.7	50.8	259
2	6.4	29.0	148
3	3.3	8.8	45
4	1.6	4.1	21
5	2.7	3.1	16
6	3.7	1.6	8
7	9.7	1.8	9
8	10.5	0.8	4

He argues that the policy-makers should concentrate their resources where both risk of poverty and accountability for poverty are high. In this case, that only occurs in the one-person households. Even though those households with large numbers have a higher risk of poverty than smaller households (excepting one-person ones), they do not constitute a big enough proportion of the total number of poor to warrant large expenditures of money on dealing with that group specifically.

Calculating percentages on the row marginals is more revealing here. It shows that the risk of poverty is high for one-person households and is also higher for large households (of 7 and 8 persons). Probably the figures reflect poor OAPs (one-person households) as one major source of poverty and large families as another separate source.

Activity 4

Because this is an experiment it is very easy to know which the dependent variable is and which the independent. The manipulated variable, here the *severity of initiation* condition, is the independent variable and its effect on *liking* is being tested (see Table 27).

Table 27 Adapted Aronson and Mills's results: percentage table

	No initiation	Severe initiation	Difference in % (no initiation/ severe initiation)
Liked group	54.0	76.0	− 22.0
Did not like group	46.0	24.0	+ 22.0
Total	100% ($N = 50$)	100% ($N = 50$)	

I conclude that there is a 22 per cent difference between the girls who were let into the group without any initiation and those who were made to read the passage of prose before they joined, in the extent to which they liked the group. So something about the reading of passages of florid prose has an effect on the way in which you perceive the group that enforces such initiation conditions. But I am not absolutely happy that it was because the girls actually *suffered* from doing this. It may be that they were in fact sexually aroused and this made them like the group discussions more. I will not conclude that the hypothesis is true until I see this experiment replicated in different situations, with different operationalizations of the word 'suffer' (recall Block 1 for 'operationalization').

Activity 5

Several different collapses would be possible, and which you used would depend on your theories about the *way* in which religion is likely to influence voting. For example, you might have no particular theory and just want to reduce the data to manageable proportions. In this case you might single out the largest categories to be shown separately and add the rest into an 'others' category, thus:

Church of England/Scotland	621
Roman Catholic	108
Other	120
None, atheist, humanist, agnostic, don't know or no answer	117

If your theory required a contrast between 'catholic' and 'protestant', you might decide to take:

Catholic (Roman, Greek Orthodox, Russian Orthodox)	110
Protestant (C of E, non-conformist)	732
Other religions (non-christian)	7
None, agnostic or no answer	117

However, you should note that this is really a three-category recoding; the 'other religions' line contains so few cases that you could not say anything reliable about the voting behaviour of such people. In general it is better to avoid creating very small categories.

90

Activity 6

Since we expect age to have an influence on voting, rather than voting to influence how old people are, age is the independent variable and vote is the dependent variable. Therefore, we want to construct a percentage table with the percentages adding up to 100 within the categories of the independent variable, here age (Table 28).

Table 28   Cross-tabulation of vote by age-percentage table

	Labour	Conservative	Total
Old	58.8	41.2	100% (N = 51)
Young	75.0	25.0	100% (N = 120)
Difference in % (old/young)	− 16.2	+ 16.2	

Age and vote are associated since there is a 16.2 per cent difference between old and young people in the way they vote. But the degree of association is not so strong that we can completely predict which way someone will vote by knowing how old they are.

Even if we could, this would not necessarily mean that age as such *causes* people to vote the way they do. It may be that people born in different generations have grown up to expect different political styles of government, which in turn affects the way they vote. Or it may be that regardless of what generation you were in, there is something inherent to the process of growing older that you grow more conservative, and thus tend to vote for the Conservative party. If the latter cases were true, then perhaps we could argue that age was indeed one of the causes of the way people voted. But in the first case of it being a generational effect, we would say that age did not cause vote directly, but it did through causing membership of a particular cohort, which in turn caused exposure to particular political events, which in turn had a causal effect on the way one voted. I do not think that age 'explains' vote because I do not find the reason for the correlation immediately obvious. I will continue to probe this relationship until I come up with a satisfactory explanation of why it is that younger people should vote differently from old. (For further discussion, see Appendix 2.)

Activity 7

When I did this I got the following result (Table 29).

Table 29

Red	Black	d
0.1	0.1	0
0.3	0.1	+ 0.2
0.1	0.2	− 0.1
0.6	0.1	+ 0.5
0.2	0.2	0
0.6	0.3	+ 0.3
0.5	0.4	+ 0.1
0.1	0	+ 0.1
0.3	0.4	− 0.1
0.3	0.1	+ 0.2

In other words, my first ten cuts of the red pile produced one face card, and so did the first ten cuts of the black one, so there was no difference. Next time, however, I turned up three face cards in the red pile and only one in the black, giving a *d* of + 0.2 (and so on). The resulting histogram (Figure 8) is not at all normal.

Figure 8

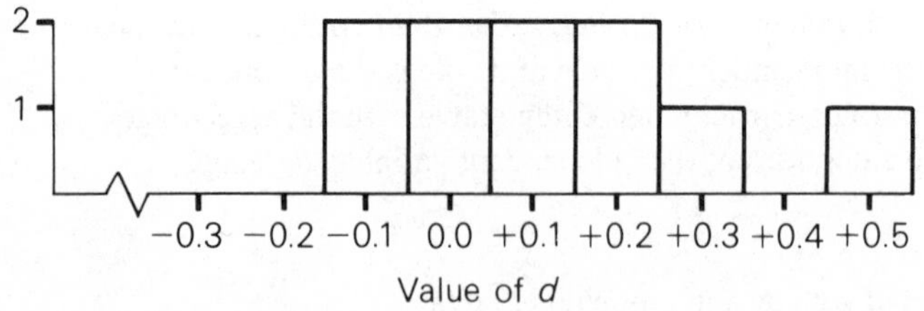

No. of times value of d occurred
2
1
−0.3 −0.2 −0.1 0.0 +0.1 +0.2 +0.3 +0.4 +0.5
Value of d

There are two reasons why this is not normal:

1 We were only calculating the d on sample size 10; the sample size needs to be larger than this before the distribution of sample d's is smooth and approximately normal.

2 We only did this experiment 10 times; in other words we only calculated 10 d's, whereas the theoretical sampling distribution is based on the idea of drawing an *infinite* number of random samples. Sampling theory tells us that the resulting distribution would have looked like this (Figure 9).

Figure 9

Frequency of occurrence of d
−10 −9 −8 −7 −6 −5 −4 −3 −2 −1 0 +1 +2 +3 +4 +5 +6 +7 +8 +9 +10
d

Activity 8

For Table 19

$p_1 = 0.427 \quad 1 - p_1 = 0.573 \quad n_1 = 143$

$p_2 = 0.0405 \quad 1 - p_2 = 0.595 \quad n_2 = 84$

Standard error is:

$$\sqrt{\frac{p_1(1-p_1)}{n_1} + \frac{p_2(1-p_2)}{n_2}}$$

$$= \sqrt{\frac{0.245}{143} + \frac{0.241}{84}}$$

$$= \sqrt{0.00171 + 0.00287}$$

$$= \sqrt{0.00458}$$

or 0.068

For a 95 per cent confidence interval we require an interval of $\pm$ 2 standard errors or $\pm$ 0.136.

The population D lies within the interval:

0.022 ± 0.136

This means that 0 is contained in the interval estimate and that the d, found from sample data could have arisen purely from sampling fluctuations. There may well be no association in the population and this is the safest conclusion to draw.

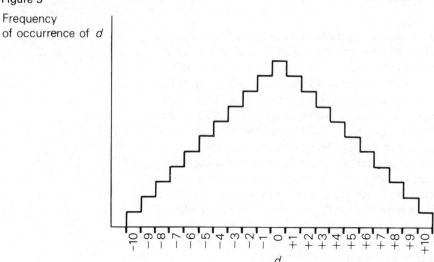

Activity 9

(a)   I presented the data in a tricky form to make you think about the anatomy of a four-fold table, but it is not all that hard to get the figures.

(i)   Lay out the table and fill in the known numbers:

Table 30

| | Respondent's class identification | | Total |
	working, lower	middle, upper	

Father's education
  8 grades or more
  Less than 8 grades
	219	303	

Total		547	1 082=N =No answer, inapplicable 1 499=Sample size

(ii)   Get as many missing numbers as possible by simple addition or subtraction:

Total 8 grades or more $= 219 + 303 = 522$
Less than 8 grades *and* middle, upper $= 547 - 303 = 244$
No answer or inapplicable $= 1499 - 1082 = 417$
Total working or lower $= 1082 - 547 = 535$

(iii)   Add them to the table:

	−	+	Total
+ −	219	303 (244)	(522)
Total	(535)	547	1 082 (417) 1 499

(iv)   Then get the last two numbers by subtraction:

	−	+	Total
+ −	219 ((316))	303 (244)	(522) ((560))
Total	(535)	547	1 082=N (417) =No answer, inapplicable 1 499=Sample size

(b) $547/1082 = 0.506$
$535/1082 = 0.494$

50.6 per cent place themselves in the middle or upper classes, 49.4 per cent place themselves in the working or lower classes.

(c)   I would decide on respondent's class as the dependent and father's education as the independent variable. In my opinion if educational levels went up, class placement of the future generation *might* change, but changes in class identification could not have any effect on parental educational levels.

(d) $303/522 = 0.580$
$244/560 = 0.436$
$$d = 0.580 - 0.436 = +0.144 \,(\pm 0.088)$$

(e)   Persons from better educated families are more likely to place themselves in the middle or upper classes.

References

ARONSON, E. and CARLSMITH, L. M. (1968) 'Experimentation in social psychology', in Lindzey, G. and Aronson, E. (eds) *Handbook of social psychology,* Vol. 2, Reading, Mass., Addison-Wesley.

EHRENBERG, A. S. C. (1975) *Data reduction,* London, John Wiley.

FIEGEHEN, G. C. (1977) *Poverty and progress in Britain 1953–73,* Cambridge, Cambridge University Press.

GOLDTHORPE, J. H. and LLEWELLYN, C. (1977) 'Class mobility in modern Britain: three theses examined', *Sociology*, Vol. 2, No. 2.

LEOTHER, H. J. and McTAVISH, D. G. (1974) *Descriptive statistics for sociologists,* Boston, Allyn and Bacon.

RUNCIMAN, W. G. (1972) *Relative deprivation and social justice,* London, Penguin.

SMITH, D. M. (1975) 'National wealth and infant mortality', reprinted in Wilson, M. J. (ed.) (1979) *Social and educational research in action: a book of readings,* London, Longman/The Open University Press (Course Reader).

Part 3   Hypothesis Testing

Prepared by John Bynner, John Murphy and R.J. Sapsford for the Course Team

Block 6   Part 3

Contents

Aims

In Part 2 of the Block we considered one kind of statistical inference: assessing likely population values. This final Part takes the argument a stage further by showing how you can use statistics inferentially to test research hypotheses. It introduces you to the logic of hypothesis testing and to the kinds of error which can be made when we are basing judgements about a population on what we have found out about a relatively small sample of it – the normal situation of the social researcher. It also introduces a range of statistical techniques which are commonly used in quantitative social research and with which you need to be familiar. (You will probably find some of them very useful when you come to analyse your Survey Project data.)

Study Guide

We recommend that you treat this as a basic teaching text, working through the examples in the order in which they are given and attempting all the exercises; there is no other way to acquire facility at calculations than by actually doing them.

There is no set reading for this Part. You will, however, find the articles by Kish and Selvin and Stuart (Principles and Procedures Reader) useful extensions of the text.

Recommended Reading

KISH, L. (1959) 'Some statistical problems in research design', in Bynner, J. and Stribley, K. M. (eds) (1979) *Social research: principles and procedures*, Ch. 8 (Course Reader).

SELVIN, H. C. and STUART, A. (1966) 'Data-dredging procedures in survey analysis', in Bynner, J. and Stribley, K. M. (eds) (1979) *Social research: principles and procedures*, Ch. 21 (Course Reader).

1 Introduction to Statistical Inference

1.1 In Block 3, and again in the previous Part of this Block, we encountered one type of statistical inference: how to *estimate* the characteristics of a population (*parameters*) from the data provided by one sample (*sample statistics*). In this Part of the Block we are going to focus our attention on the other main use of statistical inference – *hypothesis testing*.

statistical inference.
parameter, sample statistics

hypothesis testing

1.2 You will remember from Block 2, Part 1 that in carrying out any piece of research we start with a question about the causes of an observed phenomenon. For example, we might begin with the question 'What causes poor reading attainment in children?'. We then put forward a hypothesis to answer the question, for example, 'family background influences poor reading attainment'. Finally we recast the hypothesis in operational terms: 'Parents' income is related to children's scores on the Spooncer reading test' or 'There is a *positive correlation* between parents' income and children's scores on the Spooncer reading test'.

1.3 Having specified an operational hypothesis in this form we can then collect data to test it. There are two steps involved. The first is to describe the data statistically: we summarize our observations in terms of statistical indices which enable us to analyse the interrelationships of the variables to which the hypothesis refers. The second step brings in statistical inference: we want to know to what extent the results of our descriptive analysis can be generalized to cover the wider population from which the sample was drawn.

1.4 The distinction between these two stages in hypothesis testing is sometimes not easily grasped and often causes confusion. The point to be noted is that we can test a hypothesis by analysing data collected from any one example. But such a hypothesis is of limited use unless we can generalize it. In the physical sciences this problem normally does not occur. If we establish a relationship between the temperature of an iron bar and its length, we are on reasonably safe ground to conclude that the relationship will hold for *any* iron bar. But with data collected from a *sample* of observations as in social research we can establish generalizations of a probabilistic kind only. We can specify the *probability* that an apparent difference in sample data does not represent a real difference in the population from which the sample comes, but no more. A study of one school may tell us a great deal about the children who attend it, and this may well be all we want to know as a basis for certain decisions that we have to take in the school. However, once we wish to generalize our findings outside the school to the wider population of school children, we can do so only in terms of probability.

1.5 But what do we mean by probability? Perhaps the easiest way to conceive it is to think in terms of betting odds. A roulette wheel has thirty-six numbers on it. On average how many times would we expect any number to occur (a) in 360 spins (b) in 36 spins? In the first case you should have answered ten and in the second the answer is one. On average over a large number of spins we might expect each number to occur once in every thirty-six spins. This fact is reflected in the odds a casino gives the gambler against the bet on a number. If the gambler bets on a number which wins, he or she receives thirty-five times the size of the bet. In other words the casino knows that the *odds against* the number coming up by chance are 35 to 1. The *probability* (designated p) of any number's occurrence in any one spin is $\frac{1}{36}$ or 0.028.

1.6 Exactly the same principle applies in the testing of statistical hypotheses in educational research. In this case the researcher is interested in the probability of a particular sample result occurring by chance. He wants to know the odds *against* a chance occurrence. If the odds against occurrence by chance are greater than a certain figure, he decides that his result is *statistically significant*. In

statistically significant

practice he focuses his attention on certain fixed probability levels, which you will repeatedly encounter in research reports. These specify the probability of a chance occurrence of findings for a sample. The largest probability he generally considers is $p = 0.05$, or 5 occurrences by chance in 100: the odds *against* a chance occurrence are 95 to 5 or 19 to 1. A smaller probability he often considers is $p = 0.01$ or 1 occurrence by chance in 100: the odds *against* a chance occurrence are 99 to 1. Even smaller still is $p = 0.001$ or 1 occurrence by chance in 1000: the odds *against* chance occurrence are 999 to 1. In general the *less* the probability of a chance result (low p value) the more confidence the researcher has in his results.

1.7   To give these figures more substance let us look at an example of some actual research results. Haddon and Lytton (1968) wanted to test the hypothesis that children's performance on certain tests of divergent thinking would be better in primary schools which used 'informal' teaching methods than in those which used 'formal' teaching methods. They identified two similar schools of each type and compared the mean scores on several tests of divergent thinking in the two pairs of schools. Their results are shown in Table 1.

Table 1   Mean values of divergent thinking test scores in two types of school

Test	Formal schools	Informal schools	Difference	p
Verbal reasoning	101·75	101·14	−0·61	NS
Circles	10·55	12·80	2·25	< 0·01
Vague shape of dots	5·82	7·50	1·68	< 0·01
Block printing	6·19	10·35	4·16	< 0·01
Uses for a shoebox	5·78	7·25	1·47	< 0·05
Problems which might arise in taking a bath	10·32	11·81	1·49	NS
Imaginative stories	12·48	14·15	1·67	< 0·05
Sample size (n)	104	107		

1.8   The first two columns of figures in the table show the mean scores on the tests in each type of school. The third column shows the difference in these mean values. (Alternatively, Haddon and Lytton could have dichotomized the scores on each test and presented differences in percentages of children with 'high scores' as opposed to 'low scores' between the two schools. This is the *d*-statistic which you encountered in Part 2 of this Block.)

d-statistic

SAQ 1
What would be the main disadvantage of dichotomizing?

1.9   The final column of the table, which is our main interest, presents probability values or significance levels. These show the odds against the observed difference having occurred by chance. You can see from this table that Haddon and Lytton used two significance levels to define significant differences in the mean scores on the two tests: $p < 0.05$ and $p < 0.01$. (The sign simply means a probability of less than the figure following it, i.e. $p < 0.05$ signifies the probability of a chance occurrence of *less than* 0.05 or odds against a chance occurrence of *more than* 19 to 1.) You can see from the table that Haddon and Lytton set this probability as the lowest significance level that they were prepared to accept. Differences with a probability of a chance occurrence larger than 0.05 are designated 'not statistically significant' (NS).

1.10   We can see from their results that all except one of the divergent thinking tests, 'problems which might arise in taking a bath', were significant at the 0.05

level or above; whereas the verbal reasoning test which produced a slightly higher score in the formal schools than in the informal schools, showed a non-significant difference. Values of p and odds against chance are two ways of expressing statistical significance. You will also encounter references to 'significance levels'. In this case the probability is expressed as a percentage, for example $p < 0.05$ becomes the 5 per cent significance level and $p < 0.01$ becomes the 1 per cent significance level.

SAQ 2

These different methods of expressing statistical significance are summarized in Table 2. Try to complete the last two columns yourself.

Table 2   Indications of statistical significance

Level	Probability limits	Frequency of a chance occurrence	Significance levels	Odds against a chance occurrence
Low	$p < 0.05$	5 in 100	5%	19 : 1
↓	$p < 0.01$	1 in 100	1%	49 : 1
High	$p < 0.001$	1 in 1000	.1%	999 : 1

1.11   We can usefully extend our analogy between gambling and statistical hypothesis testing a bit further. In fact, by setting a particular significance level the researcher is gambling that he or she will distinguish chance results (ones which do not accurately reflect the state of affairs in the population) from genuine ones. If he sets his level too high, i.e. a very *small* probability value, then he may decide that a difference is a chance result when it is in fact a genuine one. If he sets it too low he may be in danger of accepting a result which has arisen by chance. The outcome of such a gamble, more commonly known as a statistical decision, can have serious consequences. Suppose a vast amount of money is to be invested in a new teaching method and a researcher is asked to find out whether it improves children's attainment. If in comparing the results of two groups of children, one group which has experienced the new method and the other which has not, he sets his significance level too high (e.g. $p < 0.0001$) he may conclude that the teaching method is ineffective – whereas in fact it does provide a small but genuine improvement. On the other hand if he sets his significance level too low (e.g. $p < 0.1$) he may decide that his teaching method is worth introducing, whereas in fact the improvement it appears to produce is actually a chance effect. In this case his conclusions might lead to the expenditure of a vast amount of money with fruitless results.

1.12   All this goes to show that significance testing in social and educational research needs to be tempered with a good deal of personal judgement and commonsense. In common with the general strategy of science, the usual practice is to set a sufficiently high significance level to *minimize* the possibility of accepting chance results. But by doing this there is always a danger of overlooking a genuine result. A good researcher will keep this in mind when testing statistical hypotheses using a particular significance level, and looks for evidence for general trends in results as well as statistically significant or statistically insignificant findings.

1.13   To underline this last point let us look again at Table 1. If Haddon and Lytton had used only one test, 'problems which might arise in taking a bath', to test their hypothesis that informal teaching methods increase divergent thinking abilities in children, they would have been forced to a negative conclusion. However, by using a battery of tests they were able to see that although the difference for 'problems which might arise in taking a bath' was statistically insignificant it was in the same general direction as for the other tests. In other words this result gave them additional support for their main hypothesis.

2 The Statistical Hypothesis

2.1 The previous section should give you an idea of what hypothesis testing in research is primarily about. But to understand it properly we need to know a good deal more about its foundations. We need to know what a statistical hypothesis is, how we get it into a form for testing and where the probability values that we use to confirm or refute it come from.

2.2 Statistical hypotheses are concerned with the relationships between the *population parameters* of variables. The relationship may be expressed in two forms. On the one hand, we might say that the correlation between, for example, level of education and level of income is *significantly* greater than zero. If our index of relationship is the *product moment correlation coefficient*, we want to know the chances of its being greater than zero in the total population. On the other hand, we might state the hypothesis in terms of significant differences between groups. For example, we might want to know whether a difference in the mean age of leaving school between two samples of people from high and low income families is likely to be greater than zero in the total population. (Or, like Haddon and Lytton in the example given above, we might want to find out whether the difference in mean scores on tests of divergent thinking between children attending 'formal' and 'informal' schools is likely to be different from zero in the total population.) Another way of looking at it is to imagine that we construct a 'model population' in which the difference or correlation does *not* exist. From statistical theory we can then work out the probability that the differences (or correlations) we have actually observed could have arisen by chance in random samples from such a population. If this probability is sufficiently small we reject the model and conclude that the differences are genuine. We infer that the random samples for which the difference has occurred have not been drawn from the *same* population, but from two *different* populations.

population parameter

product moment correlation coefficient

2.3 So we can test hypotheses about the relationships *between* variables or about *differences* between groups. Notice that in both cases what we are actually concerned with is the *relationship* between two variables. In the case of the correlation coefficient we investigate the relationship directly. In the case of differences between groups we are comparing the mean value of one variable between two or more groups defined by another variable, i.e. 'family income' or 'formality of teaching methods' as the case may be. In practice, statistical hypotheses, and the tests we employ to support or refute them, fall into two groups depending on whether they are concerned with indices of relationship or difference. But it is important to realize that their objective is primarily the same – to elucidate the relationships between variables. This means that we often have available to us more than one way of testing a statistical hypothesis. Which one we use depends on the way we choose to state our hypothesis.

2.4 This is, in effect, the first decision we have to make in hypothesis testing: what are we trying to find out? But we then need to take a further step. To see what this step is we shall stay with our difference hypothesis, but bear in mind that exactly the same considerations apply with relationship hypotheses. You will have noticed that in putting our difference hypothesis in statistical terms, we introduced the idea of zero relationship and zero difference in the population. This brings us to the important point that in statistical analysis we do not actually test the hypothesis we are advancing but its logical opposite – the *null hypothesis*. In other words we do not test the hypothesis that a population correlation or difference does exist, but instead we test the hypothesis that there is no population correlation or difference.

null hypothesis

2.5   The reasoning is based on simple logic. Suppose we hypothesize that there should be a difference in the population mean scores of boys and girls on an arithmetic test with a range of marks from 0 to 20. This hypothesis would be satisfied by any difference in the mean scores from 0 to 20. More realistically, the difference might be 3, 5, 7 or 9 marks – any of these would satisfy the hypothesis. On the other hand, if we state the hypothesis in the null hypothesis form, i.e. that no difference exists, we have only one value to deal with, zero. We can then say that the null hypothesis is refuted if any difference occurs at all. This, of course, would be a valid statement to make about differences in the total population. In practice we are generally dealing with a sample of data from the population which we use to estimate the population values of our variables. As we have seen, any estimate of a population parameter involves *sampling error*. So what we are actually doing in stating a statistical null hypothesis is saying that there is no difference between the mean values *over and above the difference brought about by random sampling error*. As we shall see later, statistical theory enables us to specify the limits of this sampling error around any estimated population value, including zero. We can thus set precise limits – significance levels – for the rejection of a null hypothesis. This is the basic principle on which all statistical tests are founded.

sampling error

2.6   Setting aside the question of sampling error for a moment, suppose we are able to reject a null hypothesis. We then have evidence for an *alternative hypothesis* that a difference does exist. This is of course the hypothesis that we are primarily interested in, but we call it the alternative hypothesis to emphasize the point that we reach it via the null hypothesis and not the other way round. Now let us complicate the issue a little more by considering two alternative forms that the alternative hypothesis can take. So far we have talked about *differences* between groups; we have not specified their direction. Suppose we have introduced an improved method of teaching arithmetic, but only half the schools in the country have employed it. Then we are on fairly safe ground to assume that children in this latter group of schools are not going to do worse on an arithmetic test than children in schools using the established methods. We can narrow down the hypothesis to say that the former group of children should do better than the latter group. The null hypothesis now states that there is no difference between the two groups of children in a *specified direction*. We call this latter type of null hypothesis a *directional null hypothesis*. It compares with a *non-directional null hypothesis* in which no indication of the direction of the difference is given.

alternative hypothesis

directional null hypothesis, non-directional null hypothesis

2.7   We can now summarize the various steps in formulating statistical hypotheses. These are set out in Figure 1. Notice that for convenience we designate the null hypothesis H_0 and the alternative hypothesis H_1.

SAQ 3
(a)   Suppose you are interested in investigating the Plowden Committee's conclusion that involving parents more fully in the life of the primary school will improve children's educational attainment. You have available to you data on reading attainment in a large number of primary schools. You also know whether each school runs a parent/teacher association (PTA). Write down a hypothesis that you might test to investigate the relationship between parental involvement with primary school and children's attainment, and then reformulate your hypothesis for statistical testing. Follow the steps set out in Figure 1.

(b)   Given the same research problem, suppose you have data on the number of PTA meetings each school holds a year. What form might your statistical hypothesis take?

Figure 1   Statistical hypothesis formulation

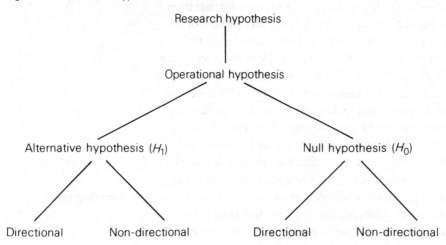

2.8   So far we have talked as if *any* difference between two mean scores might provide a case for rejecting a null hypothesis. In practice, of course, we are not concerned with just *any* indication of a difference. We make another decision about the differences which we will accept as *significant*. Again notice that for population data this consideration would apply just as much as it would for sample data. If we measure divergent thinking among all children in the country and find that those who experience informal teaching methods are only marginally better at it than those who experience formal teaching methods, investment of effort in persuading schools to adopt the informal approach would seem worthless. (This is of course assuming that we want to encourage children to think divergently!) The result has no practical significance. The question to decide is what is marginal and what is important. In other words, the practical aspects of such a decision bring in educational, political, economic, and perhaps even philosophical considerations as well as statistical ones.

2.9   With sample data we have to go a step further. Regardless of whether the results are going to be of any practical significance, we have to decide whether

Figure 2   Statistical decisions

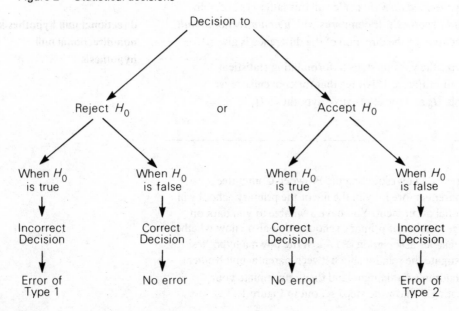

they could have arisen by chance. We have to make a decision about their *statistical significance*. As we noted earlier (section 1), this involves a decision as to what *probability level* will define a chance result. We might decide that a significant result is one for which the odds against a chance occurrence are greater than 19 to 1 ($p < 0.05$) or we might set the odds higher, say 99 to 1 ($p < 0.01$). In making such a decision we are laying ourselves open to two types of error. First we might set a significance level which is too low; we might *reject* the null hypothesis when it is in fact true. Secondly, we might set a level which is too high; we might *accept* the null hypothesis when it is in fact false. Statisticians call the first type of error *Type* 1 and the second type of error *Type* 2. The whole decision-making process is set out in Figure 2.

2.10   But how do we decide where to set our significance level? The problem is not unlike that facing the gambler playing roulette who has to decide whether to maximize his possible profits on a single number (odds of 35 to 1 against) or to opt for less by betting on, say, all red numbers as opposed to black numbers (odds of 1 to 1, or evens). As scientists, researchers generally opt for high odds; they want to minimize the possibility of rejecting a null hypothesis when it is in fact true. They consider the error of drawing a false conclusion that a relationship exists between variables more serious than the error of failing to uncover some actual relation. The point is that statistical hypothesis testing is a procedure which involves *decision*. The decision that is ultimately made depends as much on commonsense as on statistics. Statistical tests help the researcher to arrive at useful conclusions about the validity of a hypothesis. They do not provide him with validation in any absolute sense.

SAQ 4

(a)   Suppose you were given the job of finding out whether a new type of traffic-control computer decreased road accidents, so that you could advise the government whether to spend a large sum of money supplying these to local areas.

(b)   Suppose you were asked by the manufacturers to compare the efficiency of two computerized payroll systems, one of which is already in use, the other new and expensive.

(c)   Suppose you were a University lecturer who had developed a new approach to the teaching of inferential statistics which you wanted to use in future years.

In each case, you have designed an experiment to carry out the evaluation. What decisions would you have to take when examining and analysing your results? How might these differ between the three examples, and what factors would affect them? Spend five to ten minutes thinking about these questions and jot down your answers on a piece of paper.

---

3   Significance Levels

3.1   So far you have had to take the notion of significance levels on trust. You know that we express them as probabilities. When we state that a null hypothesis is rejected at the 0.05 level we are saying in effect that the probability that the sample result which led to its rejection could have occurred by chance is less than 0.05; it could have occurred by chance less than 5 times in 100; the odds against its chance occurrence are more than 19 to 1. But where do these probability levels come from and how do we actually apply them in social and educational research? To find out we have to introduce the idea of the *theoretical probability distribution*.

theoretical probability distribution

3.2   Theoretical probability distributions are the mathematical models against which we set our research observations. They enable us to state with a fair degree of precision the probability that a particular observation – say the mean score on a school test obtained from a sample of children – has occurred by chance. The basic reasoning that lies behind a probability distribution was considered briefly in Block 3, Part 4. You will recall that we introduced a very important statistical concept there – *random sampling error*. Let us retrace our steps. We reasoned that the estimate of the mean value of a variable in a population from a random sample of data contains error brought about by the sampling process. We can only specify certain limits for the estimate; we can never be certain that it is correct. We next went on to consider how to define these limits. We reasoned that if we selected a number of large samples, say with fifty or more observations in each of them, the frequencies of the mean values obtained from the samples would conform to a certain distribution. Some mean values would occur with high frequency, others with lower frequency and so on. In fact the mean values conform to the well known bell-shaped or *normal distribution* which is shown in Figure 3.

normal distribution

Figure 3   Frequency distribution of sample means

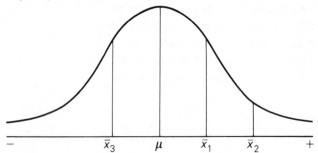

3.3   On the horizontal axis the different values of the means obtained in the random samples are shown ($\overline{X}_1$, $\overline{X}_2$, $\overline{X}_3$) around the population mean μ. The area under the curve between say, $\overline{X}_1$ and μ in Figure 3 represents the relative frequency (probability) of finding a mean as extreme in the plus direction as $\overline{X}_1$ in a series of random samples from a population whose true mean is μ. (As we shall see, this is what the table of normal distribution probabilities which is used in many statistical tests gives us.) The difference between each sampling mean value and the population mean, e.g. $\overline{X}_1 - \mu$, is the sampling error. Thinking now in terms of errors rather than mean values, you can see that at the centre of the distribution we have zero error. This occurs with maximum frequency – i.e. of all our estimates of the population mean the correct value will occur with highest frequency. As we move to the 'tails' of the curve, the errors get larger, but their frequency correspondingly decreases. In other words in our very large number of samples, the size of the error we are likely to find is *inversely* related to the number of samples in which it occurs. As the size of the error goes up, its frequency goes down. Minimum errors are likely to occur most often; maximum errors are likely to occur least often; in between we have errors of varying frequency of occurrence.

3.4   You will recall from Block 3 that the frequency distribution of sampling errors leads us directly to a definition of the sampling error of the population mean. The descriptive measure we use is the *standard deviation* of the frequency distribution of errors or *standard error*. The formula which defines the standard error is:

standard deviation, standard error

$$s_{\overline{x}} = \sqrt{\frac{\Sigma \overline{X} - \mu^2}{n}}$$

where *n* equals the number of observations in each sample for which the samples means are obtained.

106

You will further recall that as we generally have no means of knowing the population mean, nor do we have access to data from a large number of samples, we make an *estimate* of the standard error from the data collected from any one sample. The best estimate is obtained from the following formula:

$$s_{\bar{x}}(\text{estimate}) = \frac{s_x}{\sqrt{n}}$$

Here s_x is the estimated standard deviation from sample and n is the sample size.[1] Notice that the size of the standard error is inversely related to sample size. In other words the bigger the sample the smaller the standard error. As we shall see this has an important consequence for statistical hypothesis testing.

3.5 We have defined each sampling error as the difference between a sample mean value and the population mean value. Clearly, errors measured in this way will be dependent upon the size of the particular population mean we are dealing with. The bigger it is, the bigger the possible range of errors and consequently the bigger the standard error. As you know, in situations of this kind in data analysis we generally standardize our data. We transform each measurement, in this case an error, into a measurement made in terms of a single set of standard units. The most useful way of doing this is to use the standard deviation as the basic unit. We produce a set of standardized scores referred to as *z-scores* where: **z-scores**

$$z = \frac{X_i - \bar{X}}{s}$$

3.6 In this case we use the standard error itself as the basic unit. We divide each error by the standard deviation of the distribution of errors, i.e. the standard error. This transformation gives us a set of z-scores, all of which are measured in terms of standard error units – that is, we have a set of z-scores where:

$$z = \frac{X_i - \bar{X}}{s_{\bar{x}}}$$

We can now fit our distribution of sampling errors to our new scale. This is done in Figure 4.

Figure 4   Frequency distribution of sampling errors in standard error units

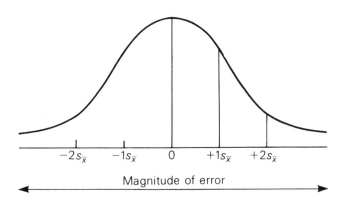

Magnitude of error

---

[1] *Note that s here is the estimated standard deviation, which has the formula (see Block 3, Part 4):*

$$s_x = \sqrt{\frac{\Sigma(X_i - \bar{X})^2}{n - 1}}$$

A simple computational formula which works directly from the raw scores is:

$$s_x = \sqrt{\left(\frac{\Sigma X_i^2 - \Sigma(\bar{X})^2}{n - 1}\right)}$$

3.7 In Block 3, Part 4 we considered the probability of errors occurring within a *specified range*. For hypothesis testing we now need to consider probabilities *outside* a certain range. We concentrate on the area at the tails of the normal distribution curve. These define our significance levels in hypothesis testing; i.e. they specify certain ranges of errors for which the probability of occurrence is less than (<) a certain size. The significance levels that we are generally interested in are $p < 0.05$ and $p < 0.01$. We can now relate these probabilities to areas of the normal distribution curve as shown in Figure 5.

Figure 5   Probability of errors outside different ranges of the mean

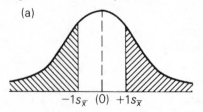
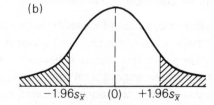
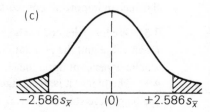

3.8 Outside the range of one standard error (the shaded area in Figure 5(a)) we have an area in the two tails of the curve equal to 0.3174 of the total area. This means that the probability of a sample mean value occurring outside the range of one standard error is less than 0.3174. Now, working backwards, let us mark off the two areas of the curve which when added together give us an area of 0.05. You can see from the curve (b) that mean values greater than 1.96 standard errors from the population mean fall into this region of the curve. In other words, their probability of occurrence is *less than* 0.05. Similarly if we mark out areas of the curve (c) which in total give an area of 0.01 we see that values greater than 2.58 standard errors from the population mean fall into this area. This is to say that their probability of occurrence is *less than* 0.01. You can see the full range of these probability regions or significance levels in the statistical tables.

SAQ 5
From the table of normal distribution probabilities in the *Statistics Booklet*, what is the probability of obtaining sample mean values which differ from the population mean by three or more standard errors?

3.9 We can now begin to see the basis for statistical hypothesis testing. As you will recall, in testing a statistical hypothesis we want to know the probability that a particular sample value, say of a correlation coefficient or a difference between means, has occurred by chance. We can now define chance as the region of error between certain specified values, for example ± 1.96 standard errors. These are known as *critical values*. If the sample value occurs outside this range its probability of occurrence by chance is *less than* 0.05. Similarly if the sample value occurs outside the range between the critical values $+2.58$ and -2.58 standard errors, its probability of occurrence by chance is *less than* 0.01.

critical values

3.10 Now let us bring these ideas together, and extend them a little further, by a simple example. Suppose we have a sample of 100 eleven-year-old children who have experienced discovery learning methods at primary school and we want to find out whether this experience has affected their performance in arithmetic as assessed by an arithmetic test. Suppose further that we are in the fortunate position of knowing the performance of all eleven-year-old children in the country on the arithmetic test. We hypothesize that the mean score on the arithmetic test for the sample will differ from the population mean score, so our *null* hypothesis is that they will not differ from each other. We decide to set out significance levels at $p < 0.05$. Our basic data are as follows:

Sample size	=	100
Mean for population	=	10
Mean for sample	=	11
Standard deviation	=	3
Estimated standard error of population mean	$= \dfrac{3}{\sqrt{100}} = 0.3$	

We can test the null hypothesis by seeing how many standard errors our observed sample mean value is from the population mean value. The value we obtain for this difference is $\dfrac{11 - 10}{0.3} = 3.33$. Now we know that all values that are more or less than 1.96 standard errors from the mean have a probability of occurrence by chance of less than 0.05. As our obtained value is 3.33 standard errors from the population mean this means that the null hypothesis is rejected.

3.11   But now let us go a step further. You will notice that in our example we have not said whether the children's experience of discovery learning methods is likely to produce an improvement or a deterioration in their arithmetic attainment. We have simply said it will produce a difference. Our hypothesis is *non-directional* (to use the terminology of section 2) and to test it we used the areas at both ends of the normal distribution. For obvious reasons we call such a test a *two-tailed test*. Suppose that we have strong grounds for believing that discovery learning methods will improve arithmetic performance. In this case we have a *directional hypothesis* and we can specify the direction in which rejection of the null hypothesis will occur. Instead of taking into account both tails of the probability distribution we now have to deal with only one – the *one-tailed test*. To find out the probabilities for rejection of this type of hypothesis we mark out the areas in the positive half of the curve equal to probabilities of 0.05 and 0.01. These are shown in Figure 6.

two-tailed test

one-tailed test

3.12   In this case to reject the null hypothesis at the 0.05 level we have to find a value that is greater than the population mean value by only 1.65 standard errors. This is the critical value. Similarly to reject the null hypothesis at the 0.01 level our sample value needs to exceed a critical value of only 2.33 standard errors. Thus our directional null hypothesis about the effect of discovery learning on arithmetic attainment is now even more strongly rejected. In other words if we can confidently state the direction of a null hypothesis we do not need such large observed differences to reject it at particular significance levels.

3.13   It should be clear from the above that stating a null hypothesis in a directional form loads the dice in favour of its rejection. For this reason many

Figure 6   One-tailed significance levels

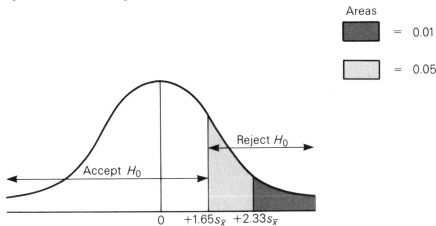

researchers opt for caution by keeping the hypothesis non-directional and consequently using a two-tailed significance test to test it. Virtually the only situations where directional tests are used are when a procedure, such as a new teaching method, has been *designed* to produce changes in a population in a particular direction, and it is extremely unlikely that it will have adverse effects. Sometimes however this caution may not be as admirable as it seems. You will remember that if we set a significance level too high there is always a danger that we accept a null hypothesis that is in fact false; that is we make a type 2 error. There might be cases then in a particular research field where a lot of evidence has accumulated about the direction of a difference to justify the use of a one-tailed test. The use of a one-tailed test makes it *easier* for us to reject a false null hypothesis.

SAQ 6

For the sample data for eight-year-old children below, can we reject at the 0.01 level (a) a non-directional null hypothesis and (b) a directional null hypothesis about the effect that parents who help their children to read have on their children's reading performance as measured by a reading test?

Sample size	=	100
Population mean reading score	=	15.0
Sample mean reading score	=	15.5
Standard deviation of reading scores	=	2

3.14 From the table of probabilities associated with the normal distribution it is possible to read off the full range of critical values for rejection of either a directional or a non-directional null hypothesis at particular significance levels. But remember that in practice most researchers work with probabilities of 0.05 and 0.01 for rejection of either type of null hypothesis: that is to say they are concerned with only four critical values, 1.96, 2.58, 1.65, 2.33. This is because the principle of statistical hypothesis testing is one of *decision*. In theory at least we should decide the significance level at which we will reject a null hypothesis *before* we test it. We then apply the test to our data to see whether the null hypothesis at this significance level is supported or refuted. Table 3 summarizes the critical values we have to exceed for rejection of each type of null hypothesis. Notice finally an important point we referred to earlier regarding the effect of sample size on statistical significance. As our critical values are numbers of standard errors, the smaller the standard error, the easier it is to achieve statistical significance. This means that in large samples relatively small and often trivial differences can be judged statistically significant. In such situations we should direct our attention more to the *size* of the difference, i.e. whether it is of substantive importance, than to whether it could have arisen by chance.

Table 3 Significance values for one-tailed and two-tailed tests

Area under the tail(s) of the probability distribution	Significance level	Two-tailed non-directional test	One-tailed directional test
0.05	$p < 0.05$	$\pm 1.96 s_{\bar{x}}$	$\pm 1.65 s_{\bar{x}}$
0.01	$p < 0.01$	$\pm 2.58 s_{\bar{x}}$	$\pm 2.33 s_{\bar{x}}$

4 Statistical Tests for Large Samples

4.1 Up to now the discussion has not taken us very far into the mechanics of statistical hypothesis testing. You have probably heard of t-tests, χ^2 tests and F-tests, or even more exotic creatures like the Mann Whitney test and the Wilcoxon test – you might wonder what our discussion has got to do with them. In fact we have not even got as far as applying the tests of difference and correlation with which section 2 was concerned. So why did we spend so much time on sampling errors?

4.2 The reason is that all statistical tests rely for their existence on the notion of sampling error. Each one consists of setting a particular sample value of a variable against a distribution of sampling errors. In fact it might be fairly said that if you can understand the idea of sampling error, you can understand statistics. If you cannot understand it you may be able to apply statistical tests by rule of thumb methods, but you will gain very little appreciation of what your results are really telling you.

4.3 But why do we need so many tests? The reason is to do with the different types of data and sampling situations with which we have to deal in social and educational research. We may have large samples of data, for which we want to assess the significance of the difference between mean values or the significance of a correlation coefficient. We use the unit normal distribution or z significance test in these situations. On the other hand we may have two small samples or more than two small samples for which we want to establish differences. We use the t-test and F-test in these two situations respectively. (The F-test will be considered in Block 7.) In another situation we may have observations of human characteristics all of which fall into discrete categories without any measurement scale attached. We might have the number of people living in different regions of the country or the numbers of children with blue eyes, brown eyes and so on. In these cases to test hypotheses about the relationships between the different characteristics we use the chi square (χ^2) test. Finally we might have situations where we have no idea what the distribution of the characteristics would be like in the total population and no idea what its parameters might be. Furthermore we might feel that although we have a rudimentary measurement scale for our variables, it departs so far from the equal interval scale that the arithmetic operations involved in statistical tests are inappropriate. In these situations we sometimes resort to what are known as *non-parametric* tests of which the Mann Whitney and Wilcoxon tests are examples. **non-parametric**

4.4 Before moving on, a further word about this last type of test is in place here. The trouble with non-parametric tests is that they are generally less *powerful* than the earlier ones in our list; that is to say, they are less likely to detect a significant difference or correlation at a particular probability level. There has been considerable debate in recent years about their value in data analysis. After the early 'flight into non-parametric statistics' the move now seems to be to avoid them as far as possible almost regardless of any violation of assumptions about data on which the more powerful *parametric* statistical tests depend. This is because the parametric tests are far more 'robust' under different conditions than was originally realized. We shall not consider non-parametric tests here. You are likely to encounter them frequently in research literature, however, so they are included in Table 4, which lists some of the most common tests and their principal applications. Further information on non-parametric tests may be obtained from statistical textbooks (such as McNemar, 1962; Siegel, 1956; Guilford and Fruchter, 1973) or from other Open University courses. **power** **parametric**

4.5 Let us now consider some of the main parametric tests via the situations in which we apply them. Let us start by considering statistical hypotheses which are an extension of those we investigated in the last section. We shall stay for the time being with large samples, by which we mean samples in excess of fifty observations, and definitely not less than thirty. In between thirty and fifty we might test our hypotheses by these procedures but we need to interpret the results with caution. The hypotheses we shall be investigating are those concerned with differences between mean values (e.g. of test scores) obtained from different samples of a population and with the existence of relationships between variables as determined by the product moment correlation coefficient.

Table 4   Commonly used statistical tests

Null hypothesis	Test

Means, proportions etc. of *two* samples do not differ significantly	Parametric, 'uncorrelated' samples*:
	   Large sample = z (normal distribution)
	   Small sample = t test for uncorrelated means
	 Parametric, 'correlated' samples*: t test for correlated means
	 Non-parametric, 'uncorrelated' samples*:
	   Mann-Whitney U test†
	 Non-parametric, 'correlated' samples*:
	   Wilcoxon matched pairs test†

Means of *several* samples do not differ significantly	Parametric: Analysis of variance Non-parametric: Friedman one-way analysis of variance†

Scores on two variables are unrelated or uncorrelated	Parametric:
	   Analysis of variance
	   Regression
	   Product moment correlation coefficient (r) } where categories can be ordered
	 Non-parametric:
	   Spearman rank order correlation (r_s)
	   Chi square (χ^2) — where categories cannot be ordered

† not taught in this course. (Some of the other tests are first introduced in Block 7.)
* More powerful tests may be used where the design of the experiment or survey cuts down individual variance by taking repeated measurements on the same individual or by exact matching of subjects in two samples on relevant characteristics (yielding, in statistical jargon, *correlated means*).

4.6   In the last section the hypotheses we tested were concerned with the difference between a sample mean value of a variable and the population mean value. In practice we rarely have information about population parameters. What we do have is information about two or more samples from the population. Our hypotheses thus relate to differences between population mean values from sample estimates of each of them. For example, like Haddon and Lytton (1968) we might want to know whether children who attend schools that employ informal teaching methods have significantly higher scores on tests of divergent thinking than those who attend schools that employ formal teaching methods. Or more simply we might want to find out whether ten-year-old children who attend schools in one London borough have a higher or lower reading attainment than those who attend schools in another borough.

4.7   To see what is involved in testing such a hypothesis let us look at some typical research data for London boroughs. Suppose that we have data on reading attainment as assessed by a reading test from random samples of ten-year-old

Table 5   Data on reading in two London boroughs

	Borough 1	Borough 2
Sample size (n)	64	49
Mean reading score ($\overline{X}$)	35	30
Standard deviation (s_x)	8	6

children in two London boroughs. We want to find out whether the children in the two boroughs differ significantly with respect to the test. The data we need to decide the matter are set out in Table 5.

4.8 Our null hypothesis states that there is no significant difference between the mean reading scores in the two London boroughs. Notice that we are not specifying the direction of the difference, just that no significant difference exists. As we saw at the beginning of section 2 in these cases what we want to know is whether the samples can be considered to come from the same population – null hypothesis confirmed – or whether the samples can be considered to come from different populations – null hypothesis rejected. The principle involved in testing the null hypothesis is exactly the same as the one employed in the previous section. What we have to do is establish the *probability* that the observed difference is greater than would be expected by chance. Once again chance differences are defined in terms of standard errors. So the statistic we need for our significance test relates the observed difference to the *standard error of the difference*. In fact we need to work out a *z* value. It is defined as:

$$z = \frac{(\bar{X}_1 - \bar{X}_2) - (\mu_1 - \mu_2)}{s_{d\bar{x}}} = \frac{\bar{X}_1 - \bar{X}_2 - 0}{s_{d\bar{x}}}$$

where $s_{d\bar{x}}$ is the standard error of the difference between means.
Notice that we include the value 0 in the formula to underline the point that under the null hypothesis the population difference between the means $(\mu_1 - \mu_2)$ is zero. Our difference between sample means is $35 - 30 = 5$. All we need now to work out the value of *z* is a figure for the standard error of a difference between means, i.e. the denominator in the expression for *z*. This is given by the formula below:

$$s_{d\bar{x}} = \sqrt{s_{\bar{x}_1}^2 + s_{\bar{x}_2}^2}$$

where $s_{\bar{x}_1}$ and $s_{\bar{x}_2}$ are the standard errors of each of the population means. First we estimate the values of $s_{\bar{x}_1}$ and $s_{\bar{x}_2}$ using the formula we encountered in section 2. We have:

$$s_{\bar{x}_1} = \frac{8}{\sqrt{64}} = 1$$

and

$$s_{\bar{x}_2} = \frac{6}{\sqrt{49}} = 0.86$$

from which we obtain the estimated standard error of the difference:

$$s_{d\bar{x}} = \sqrt{(1)^2 + (0.86)^2} = \sqrt{1.74} = 1.32$$

We can now work out the value of *z*:

$$z = \frac{5}{1.32} = 3.78$$

4.9 To test the null hypothesis of no difference between the means, we compare this value of *z* with critical values at particular significance levels in the unit normal distribution. Supposing we set our significance level at 0.05. We know that the critical value of *z* at this significance level in a two-tailed test is 1.96. As our obtained value exceeds this we can reject the null hypothesis. Similarly if we set our significance level at 0.01 we exceed the critical value 2.58. So again at this significance level the null hypothesis is rejected. We can conclude that there is a significant difference in reading attainment between the two London boroughs.

4.10 Similar considerations apply to testing the significance of the *d*-statistic – the percentage difference – described in Part 2. Let us suppose, for example, that in Borough 1 fifty per cent of the sample achieved a pass-mark at the reading test, while only forty per cent passed in Borough 2.

So $d = 10$ per cent (or 0.10, expressed as a proportion).

$$s_d = \sqrt{p_c q_c \left(\frac{1}{n_1} + \frac{1}{n_2} \right)}$$

where p_c is the overall proportion passing $= \dfrac{(0.50 \times 64) + (0.40 \times 49)}{64 + 49}$

$$= 0.457$$

$q_c = 1 - p_c$

and n_1 and n_2 are the two sample sizes.

So,

$$s_d = \sqrt{(0.457 \times 0.543) \times \left(\frac{1}{64} + \frac{1}{49} \right)} = 0.0945$$

Then

$$z = \frac{0.10}{0.0945} = 1.06 \text{ (not significant)}$$

In this case we could not reject the null hypothesis with any reasonable degree of confidence. However, setting the pass-mark at some other level might well have produced a significant difference; as was noted in Part 2, different 'collapses' produce different sizes of d (and also of s_d). In general it is best, when using the d-statistic, to dichotomize at the mean or median unless you have very good theoretical reasons for doing otherwise. This helps you to avoid the charge that you have picked an unusual division-point specifically in order to find a significant difference.

SAQ 7

The table below gives the hypothetical results of a survey of income in two London boroughs:

Table 6

Income does not exceed	Borough 1	Borough 2	Total
£1 000 per year	100	400	500
£5 000 per year	700	300	1 000
£10 000 per year	100	900	1 000
£20 000 per year	50	350	400
£50 000 per year	30	30	60
Income in excess of			
£50 000	20	20	40
Sample size	1 000	2 000	3 000

Test the significance of income differences between these two boroughs, using the d-statistic as an indicator of the difference.

4.11 Just as we can determine whether a difference in mean scores on one variable is statistically significant, we can also determine whether the value of a correlation coefficient between two variables is statistically significant. Basically the procedure is the same; we want to know whether the sample estimate of our population correlation is significantly different from a population correlation of zero. For example, Entwistle and Nisbet (1972) present correlations between certain characteristics of different groups of students and their academic performance at colleges and university. For a sample of 161 men at colleges of education the correlation between extraversion and academic performance was −0.21, and the correlation between hours studying and academic performance was 0.15. How do we find out whether these correlations are likely to have occurred by chance? Let us set a significance level of $p < 0.01$. Again the first thing we have to do is find the standard error of a correlation coefficient r. This is given by the simple formula $s_r = \dfrac{1}{\sqrt{n}}$. So in this case the standard error equals $\dfrac{1}{\sqrt{161}} = 0.079$. Again, we can work out a z value for our obtained correlation, i.e.

$$z = \frac{r}{s_r}$$

Thus in the first case for the correlation between academic performance and extraversion we have:

$$z = \frac{-0.21}{0.079} = -2.66$$

In the second case for the correlation between hours studying and academic performance we have:

$$z = \frac{0.15}{0.079} = 1.90$$

as our critical value for z ($p < 0.01$) is ± 2.58, the null hypothesis is just rejected for extraversion and accepted for hours studying. We can therefore conclude tentatively that extraversion is just significantly correlated with academic performance, but that hours studying and academic performance are possibly unrelated.

4.12   Unfortunately to test hypotheses about correlations in general, the situation is not so simple. Whether we can apply the normal probability distribution to the sampling errors of a correlation coefficient depends first on the size of r in the population and secondly on the size of the sample for which it is computed. For large values of r in the population, the distribution of sampling errors is no longer normal. Generally speaking if we are dealing with a correlation greater than 0.5, we have to adopt another procedure. Once again a data transformation comes to our rescue. This time we transform our correlations to a normally distributed statistic known as z which was devised by the statistician R. A. Fisher. The equation of this function is a complex one and beyond the scope of this course. Conversion tables are provided, however, in your *Statistics Booklet* which allow you simply to look up the value of z associated with a given value of r. Then all you have to do is to divide this z by its standard error

Fisher's z

$$\left(s_z = \frac{1}{\sqrt{n-3}} \right)$$

to obtain the kind of z that you can look up in the table of normal probability values.

SAQ 8
The table overleaf shows the correlations Entwistle and Nisbet found between personality characteristics and academic performance of fifty female students at polytechnics. Indicate in the column at the right-hand side of the table whether the correlations are significant at the 0.05 level.

Table 7

Characteristic	Correlation with academic performance	Whether significant at $p < 0.05$ level
Academic aptitude	0·08	NO
Motivation	0·26	YES
Study methods	0·31	YES.
Exam technique	0·07	NO
Self hard working	0·18	YES.
Hours studying	0·30	YES
Extraversion	0·06	NO
Neuroticism	−0·41	YES

5 Difference Tests for Small Samples

5.1 In the previous section the hypotheses we investigated all involved data from a large sample of informants. With the exception of Fisher's z statistic we cannot use the normal probability distribution to test hypotheses from samples of observations less than thirty. The reason is that, for samples as small as this, the sampling errors of any statistic such as a mean value are no longer normally distributed. But suppose we wanted to test hypotheses on such samples. To do so we have to employ what are known as small sample statistical tests. One of the most important of these is known as *Student's* t-*test*.   **Student's *t*-test**

5.2 Many researchers use the *t*-test for samples of any size, for the simple reason that above a sample size of fifty the critical value of z and t converge. The main difference between z and t is that although z for large samples is always normally distributed any t distribution is only one of a family of small sample probability distributions, each of which depends on the sample size. But in fact to say 'sample size' is not strictly correct. The crucial issue with the t distribution is the number of *degrees of freedom* which the sampling error is calculated. As you   **degrees of freedom**
will recall from Block 3, Part 4, in the case of a sample estimate of the population standard deviation, s_x, the squared deviations from the mean $(X - \bar{X})^2$ are divided by $n - 1$ before taking the square root, i.e.

$$s_x = \sqrt{\frac{\Sigma(X_i - \bar{X})^2}{n - 1}} \text{ where } n - 1 \text{ is the number of degrees of freedom.}$$

It always equals sample size minus a certain value determined by the particular application of t that we are using.

5.3 Let us consider an example of the use of the t-test using pilot data collected from thirty children. Suppose that we wanted to investigate the hypothesis that girls and boys differ in their attitudes to school as assessed by a scale measuring attitudes to school. The data we need are presented in Table 8. What do we have

Table 8   Girls' and boys' attitudes to school

	Girls (1)	Boys (2)
Sample size (n)	18	12
Mean score (X)	8·06	11·25
Standard deviation (s_x)	3·47	2·13

to do to test the null hypothesis of no difference between boys and girls on the attitudes to school scale? Our first job is to find the standard error of the difference between the mean scores. In the t distribution this is given by the following formula:

$$s_{d\overline{x}} = \sqrt{\frac{(\Sigma X_1{}^2 + \Sigma X_2{}^2)}{(n_1 + n_2 - 2)} \left(\frac{n_1 + n_2}{n_1 \, n_2}\right)}$$

This formula is not as formidable as it looks. The two principal terms under the square root sign involve the sum of the squares of the deviation scores on the attitude scale for the two samples $\Sigma X_1{}^2$ and $\Sigma X_2{}^2$ and the degrees of freedom, $n_1 + n_2 - 2$. (One degree of freedom is lost in each of the two samples.)

5.4   This is the general formula for the standard error of the difference between means in the t distribution. For the attitude data we can adjust it to accommodate the fact that we have already worked out the standard deviation for the two samples. In this case as

$$s_{x_1} = \sqrt{\frac{\Sigma X_1{}^2}{n_1 - 1}} \quad \text{and} \quad s_{x_2} = \sqrt{\frac{\Sigma X_2{}^2}{n_2 - 1}},$$

$$s_{d\overline{x}} = \sqrt{\frac{(n_1 - 1)s_{x_1}^2 + (n_2 - 1)s_{x_2}^2}{(n_1 + n_2 - 2)} \left(\frac{n_1 + n_2}{n_1 \, n_2}\right)}$$

Substituting our values for s_{x_1}, s_{x_2}, n_1 and n_2 in the formula, we have:

$$s_{d\overline{x}} = \sqrt{\frac{[17 \times (3.47)^2] + [11 \times (2.13)^2]}{28} \left(\frac{30}{18 \times 12}\right)}$$

$$= \sqrt{1.26} = 1.12$$

As for z, the value of t is defined as the difference between the means divided by the standard error, i.e.

$$t = \frac{\overline{X}_2 - \overline{X}_1}{s_{d\overline{x}}} = \frac{11.25 - 8.06}{1.12} = \frac{3.19}{1.12}$$

$$= 2.85$$

5.5   We can now refer to tables of the t distribution to determine critical values for particular probability levels. But before we do this notice that we have to take into account another important point. We have a family of t distributions, each of which is identified by a particular value for the degrees of freedom. As we saw earlier, in each of the samples of data which we used to estimate the standard error we lost one degree of freedom. So the number of degrees of freedom for t is given by the sum of the two samples less 2. Thus the particular t distribution we require is for $n_1 + n_2 - 2$ degrees of freedom, i.e. 28. For our particular set of data the critical value for t with 28 degrees of freedom in a two-tailed test is 2.0 at the 0.05 level and 2.8 at the 0.01 level (see the table of critical values for the distribution in your *Statistics Booklet*). As our obtained value for t is 2.85 we can reject the null hypothesis easily at $p < 0.05$ and marginally at $p < 0.01$. We conclude cautiously that there is a statistically significant difference between the boys and girls in their attitudes to school.

5.6   There is one other application of the t distribution that we should consider. Without stating this explicitly, in all the difference tests that we have considered we have assumed that the samples are independent of each other. This simply means that the selection of children for one sample is unaffected by the selection of children for another sample. But in certain situations in educational research this is not the case. If we test one group of children twice on the same test, the two sets of observations are no longer independent of each other; they are correlated. Similarly if we select two groups of children who are matched with respect to every characteristic of known relevance – for example, we ensure that they have the same mean age – we have correlated samples. In these cases to test the hypothesis that the mean values are different we use a modified example of the t formula. This is shown below:

$$\text{Correlated sample } t = \frac{\bar{X}_d}{\sqrt{\dfrac{\Sigma X_d^2}{n\,(n-1)}}}$$

Where X_d is the difference between each pair of sample values less the mean difference $\bar{X}_d$.

5.7 As an example of the use of this formula, suppose we have tested a group of twenty children on an arithmetic test. We then carry out an intensive programme of tuition in arithmetic with the children. At the conclusion of this programme, say a fortnight later, we again test the children. We want to find out whether the teaching has led to an improvement or a deterioration in their arithmetic performance. Our null hypothesis is therefore: no difference in mean arithmetic scores between the two testing situations. Using the formula we find $t = 2.6$. Before looking up the critical value of t we have one important point to decide: how many degrees of freedom? In this case we have twenty *pairs* of observations for which the standard error in the t formula was calculated. Because we are dealing with pairs of observations and not independent samples of them we subtract one degree of freedom. Thus the number of degrees of freedom in this case is nineteen. We find that the critical value for t with nineteen degrees of freedom at the 0.05 significance level is 2.1. Our obtained value 2.6 just exceeds the critical value. Thus we can conclude that our teaching programme has produced a marginal improvement in the children's arithmetic scores.

5.8 It is important to understand that the interpretation of a t value rests on certain assumptions about the data for which it is computed. And the *smaller* the sample the more important these assumptions become. First, the population distribution of the dependent variable should be approximately normal. Secondly, the variances of the dependent variable in each sample should be approximately equal. Thirdly, the two sample sizes should be markedly different. How far we can depart from these assumptions and still legitimately use the t-test is a matter of judgement. The general rule is to interpret the results of a t-test with caution when the sample sizes are small – say twenty or less.

SAQ 9

The scores set out below were obtained from boys and girls on a peer group interest scale. Setting a significance level at 0.05, investigate the hypothesis that girls differ from boys in their attraction to peer group leisure activities.

Boys (1)	Girls (2)	
6	12	
8	13	
10	11	
4	6	
7	15	$\bar{X}_1 = 6.0$
8	9	$\bar{X}_2 = 8.33$
6	8	$s_{x_1} = 2.22$
5	12	$s_{x_2} = 3.32$
4	5	$n_1 = 13$
9	6	$n_2 = 18$
4	7	
5	7	
2	8	
	8	
	3	
	8	
	10	
	2	

---

6 Frequency Analysis

6.1   In the previous two sections the data which we used to test hypotheses were scores on tests or other variables. In many situations in educational research all we have are data in broad categories of some characteristic. For example, we might have information about the numbers of children in different classes in a school or about the numbers who have passed or failed a particular examination. Sometimes we have a measurement technique which only enables us to group children into two or three broad categories. For example, we might ask teachers to say whether children are 'good' or 'bad' at a particular school test or we might ask them to classify the children into three broad groups: 'good', 'average', 'bad'. In fact the grades the University frequently uses for tutor-marked assignments are another example of this sort of classification (A, B, C, D, F, R), though in this case and the previous one notice that there is an *order* implied in the categories. We are not dealing with simple head counts in unordered categories like region, school attended or eye colour. As you know from Block 2 these latter classifications are known as nominal scales.

6.2   The χ^2 *test* is designed primarily to deal with hypotheses that concern data in the nominal form – though in practice it is often used, perhaps wrongly, to deal with ordered categories as well. The reason why we say 'perhaps wrongly' is that the χ^2 test does not rest on any assumptions about order of magnitude in data. In consequence if we supply it to data where this information exists we are throwing the information away or 'degrading the data'. The effect of this data degradation is to lay us open to type 2 errors. The χ^2 test is less *powerful* than the other statistical tests which we have been considering so far. On the other hand if we have data reduced to two categories such as in the two by two tables in Part 2, χ^2 is the appropriate test to use. In addition it can be applied to any table of data relating two sets of unordered categories.

χ^2 **test**

6.3   So much for the dangers in χ^2 testing, now to applications. Suppose we have data for sixty children on two characteristics, each of which contains only two categories. We have the numbers of boys and girls in the group and the numbers classified as leaders and followers. We also know which are the leaders and which are the followers in each sex group. The data are shown in Table 9, an example of a *contingency table*.

contingency table

Table 9   Data on leadership among boys and girls

	Boys		Girls		Total	
Leader	10	(A)	9	(B)	19	(A + B)
Follower	15	(C)	26	(D)	41	(C + D)
Total	25	(A + C)	35	(B + D)	60	(A + B + C + D)

We want to know whether there is any difference between boys and girls in terms of their leadership propensities. Or looking at it another way, we want to know whether sex difference is *associated* with leadership.

6.4   Like the tests already described, the χ^2 test applies a 'model' to the data – but a slightly different kind of model. When comparing means we assess the probability that our two samples came from a common population as extreme but plausible random samples. Put another way, our null hypothesis says that we can *predict* the probability of our two observed readings being random deviations from a single mean, and this probability is greater than 0.05 (if we have chosen the 0.05 significance level). In the χ^2 test, our null hypothesis says that two variables are not associated – that we cannot predict scores on the one from scores on the other. We test this hypothesis by working out *expected values* for what the figures in the table would be if there were no association, then seeing how far the actual (*observed*) figures diverge from this model.

6.5   For example, in Table 9 we have twenty-five boys and thirty-five girls, nineteen leaders and forty-one followers. If there is no association between sex and leadership, then the nineteen leaders should be made up of

$$\left(19 \times \frac{25}{60}\right) = 7.9 \text{ boys and } \left(19 \times \frac{35}{60}\right) = 11.1 \text{ girls.}$$

That is, the 'leadership' row should be divided between boys and girls in the same proportions as is the 'total' row; if it is not, we would have some evidence of association. Similarly there should be $\left(41 \times \frac{25}{60}\right) = 17.1$ male followers and $\left(41 \times \frac{35}{60}\right) = 23.9$ female ones. This gives us Table 10, the *expected* values. As we can see, the expected values do not coincide with the observed ones – we observe more male leaders and fewer male followers than we would expect. Is the difference a significant one, however, or do we just happen to have drawn a sample which departs a little from being typical of a population in which the two variables are not associated?

Table 10   Expected values on leaderships among boys and girls if sex and leadership are not associated

	Boys	Girls	Total
Leader	7·9	11·1	19
Follower	17·1	23·9	41
Total	25	35	60

6.6   The formula by which we test our model takes each cell and examines the size of the difference between observed and expected values:

$$\chi_n^2 = \frac{(O - E)^2}{E}$$

where χ_n^2 is the value of χ^2 for cell A, O is the observed value, and E is the expected value. For the first cell of Table 9,

$$\chi^2 = \frac{(10 - 7.9)^2}{7.9} = 0.558.$$

The derivation of this formula need not worry you, but note (a) that the deviations from the expected value are squared, so that larger deviations make more impact, and (b) that they are expressed as proportions of the expected value – obviously a deviation of 2 is more important if the expected value is 5 than if it is 500.

6.7   We can work out similar χ^2 values for the other cells:

Girl leaders: $\chi^2 = \dfrac{(9 - 11.1)^2}{11.1} = 0.397$

Boy followers: $\chi^2 = \dfrac{(15 - 17.1)^2}{17.1} = 0.258$

Girl followers: $\chi^2 = \dfrac{(26 - 23.9)^2}{23.9} = 0.185$

Adding the four cell χ^2s together gives 1.40, the χ^2 for the whole table, which is our measure of how much the actual results differ from what we would expect on the null hypothesis of no association. Looking at Tables 9 and 10, we can see we have more male leaders than we would have expected, so if 1.40 is a significantly larger value of χ^2 than would be expected in a table of this size at, say, the 0.05 level, we would have evidence that boys are more likely than girls to become leaders.

6.8   One more task remains before we can look up the significance of our χ^2 in the table of critical χ^2 values given in your *Statistics Booklet*, and that is to make allowance for the size of the data table. As you obtain χ^2 by adding together as many figures as there are cells, you will obviously expect to get a larger χ^2 figure by chance from a table with ten cells than from Table 9, which has only four cells. Now in Table 9 we have two row totals, but only one of them is free to vary: knowing that there are 60 cases and 19 leaders, we know there *must be* 41 followers. Similarly, with 60 cases and 25 boys, there *must be* 35 girls. (This is the concept of *degrees of freedom* which has recurred throughout this text.) In fact, given one single figure (that there are ten male leaders) and the marginal totals, we can calculate how many people *must be* in each of the cells, so we say there is only one degree of freedom in the table. In general, the number of degrees of freedom in the table is given by the formula: $df = (r-1)(c-1)$, where r is the number of rows and c is the number of columns. In this case $r = 2$ and $c = 2$, so $df = 1$. Looking up our χ^2 of 1.40 in the table of critical values, for a table with one degree of freedom, we find it is too small: at the five per cent probability level we should want a χ^2 of at least 3.84 to reject the null hypothesis. Thus we have to write off our observed differences as just a random variation.

6.9   You can calculate a χ^2 for any size of table, provided the figures in the cells are not too low – a good rule of thumb is that no expected value should be smaller than five. There are two further restrictions on the use of χ^2.

(a)   Each person or reading must occur once and *only* once in the table. If, for example, you were interested in the relationship of personality to intelligence, and your personality measures classified your subjects into neurotics, stable people, extraverts and introverts, you could not use this personality classification as the rows or columns of a table: every person appears twice (as a neurotic *and* an introvert, for example). You would have to reclassify the sample into 'neurotic introverts', 'neurotic extraverts', 'stable introverts' and 'stable extraverts', so that each person appeared only once.

(b)   The two variables must be independent of each other: you may not use χ^2, for example, to compare scores of the same subjects before and after an experimental manipulation (or rather, there *is* a χ^2 test for this situation, but it is not calculated in the same way as the one given here).

SAQ 10

The table below gives data collected by Potter (1978) on the use of pedestrian subways in Milton Keynes in 1976.

Table 11   Analysis of pedestrian cross-road trips, 1976

Area	Crossing made via underpass	Crossing made via road, not underpass	Total
A Near roundabout and bus-stops	51	62	113
B Near estate roads	0	55	55
C Near school underpass	19	4	23
Total	70	121	191

Test the hypothesis that use of the underpass is heavily affected by the area in which the crossing is made.

6.10 It is important to note that with a 2 × 2 table such as Table 7 we can obtain the overall χ^2 value without having to calculate the χ^2 laboriously for each separate cell in the table. For such a table the formula becomes

$$\chi^2 = \frac{n\,(ad - bc)^2}{(a + b)\,(a + c)\,(b + d)\,(c + d)}$$

This gives us

$$\chi^2 = \frac{60\,(9 \times 15 - 10 \times 26)^2}{25 \times 35 \times 41 \times 19} = 1.37$$

which, as we have seen, is not significant at the five per cent level.

6.11 You may have noticed that the simplified formula for χ^2 from a 2 × 2 table is similar to the formula for the Ø correlation coefficient which we encountered in Block 2. In fact the two are related by the simple equation:

$$\text{Ø} = \sqrt{\frac{\chi^2}{n}}$$

This immediately points to a way of establishing the statistical significance of a Ø coefficient. We can work out Ø, convert it to χ^2 ($\chi^2 = n\text{Ø}^2$) and then compare our χ^2 with the critical value for 1 degree of freedom. This formula holds good for 2 × 2 tables in which each cell contains at least ten observations. If there are fewer than ten observations in any one cell we have to adjust them slightly by applying what is known as Yates' correction for continuity. We need not go into the reasons for it here. All we need to note is that the χ^2 formula is effectively altered in such a way that the value of χ^2 is reduced.

$$\text{Corrected } \chi^2 = \frac{n\left[\,|ad - bc| - \dfrac{n}{2}\right]^2}{(a + b)\,(a + c)\,(b + d)\,(c + d)}$$

6.12 As we had less than ten observations in one of the cells in our table relating sex and leadership, strictly speaking we should have applied Yates' correction in our calculation of χ^2. Doing this now we have more accurately

$$\chi^2 = \frac{60\,[\,|9 \times 15 - 10 \times 26| - 30]^2}{19 \times 35 \times 25 \times 41}$$

$$= 0.79 \text{ (insignificant)}$$

Note: The vertical lines $\|$ indicate that we always take the value $|ad - bc|$ as *positive.* Hence in this example $9 \times 15 - 10 \times 26$, which equals -125, becomes $+125$. Then the total value of the numerator is reduced: $125 - 30 = 95$, i.e. numerator value is 60×95^2.

SAQ 11
The table below, taken from Hoffman (1958), gives the number of laboratory groups (of four people dissimilar in personality), analysed by the number of women in the group, who were above or below the median in their preference for people in their own group rather than one of the others.

Table 12

Number of women in group	Below median in in-group preference	Above median	Total
0 or 1	10	4	14
2 to 4	2	9	11
Total	12	13	25

Calculate χ^2 with and without Yates' correction. What can you conclude on the basis of this table?

6.13 There are many applications of χ^2 other than those we have considered here. In fact the technique represents a whole branch of statistics in itself. We cannot go into the whole range here but it is worth concluding with a brief look at one common use of χ^2 known as the 'goodness of fit test'. Suppose we wanted to find whether a distribution of people across a number of categories of a characteristic differed significantly from what we might expect by chance. Let us suppose the characteristic is performance in a TMA and we have the following distribution of a random sample of students across the six grades for a particular tutor: A = 5; B = 5; C = 10; D = 5; F = 5; R = 5; Total = 35. Suppose we also know the distribution of grades among all the tutors who have marked the TMA. We want to find out whether our first tutor's marking differs significantly from the overall distribution of marks. This distribution is as follows: A = 30 per cent; B = 30 per cent; C = 10 per cent; D = 10 per cent; F = 10 per cent; R = 10 per cent. From the overall distribution we can obtain values for the expected frequencies of tutor 1 and work out values for χ^2 as shown below (Table 13).

Table 13

Grades	Tutor 1 observed frequencies	Expected frequencies	$\dfrac{(O-E)^2}{E}$		
A	5	$\dfrac{30}{100} \times 35$	$\dfrac{(5-10\cdot5)^2}{10\cdot5}$	=	2·88
B	5	$\dfrac{30}{100} \times 35$	$\dfrac{(5-10\cdot5)^2}{10\cdot5}$	=	2·88
C	10	$\dfrac{10}{100} \times 35$	$\dfrac{(10-3\cdot5)^2}{3\cdot5}$	=	12·07
D	5	$\dfrac{10}{100} \times 35$	$\dfrac{(5-3\cdot5)^2}{3\cdot5}$	=	0·64
F	5	$\dfrac{10}{100} \times 35$	$\dfrac{(5-3\cdot5)^2}{3\cdot5}$	=	0·64
R	5	$\dfrac{10}{100} \times 35$	$\dfrac{(5-3\cdot5)^2}{3\cdot5}$	=	0·64
Total	35			$\chi^2 =$	19·75

6.14 The degrees of freedom for six categories of data are $6 - 1 = 5$. We can thus compare our value of χ^2 with the critical value of this number of degrees of freedom. To be as fair as possible to the tutor we shall set a high significance level ($p < 0.01$) to minimize the risk of accepting a chance finding as genuine, i.e. concluding that the tutor's grading is biased. The critical value is 15.1 at the 0.01 level. We are thus forced to reject our null hypothesis that the distribution of our tutor's grades is no different from the distribution for all the other tutors. In other words there is a statistically significant bias in the tutor's grading.

7   Conclusions

7.1 We started this Part of the Block with the topic of statistical decision; we ended it with the mechanics of some of the tests on which statistical decisions are based. We can now draw together some final points arising from our discussion.

7.2 First to return to our initial consideration, it should be obvious to you that statistical tests do not provide any panacea for establishing scientific truth. All they can do is guide the investigator to the conclusions that may be useful. First the investigator has to decide what type of conclusions he wants to draw. This decision as to the hypothesis he wants to test may be influenced by the state of knowledge in a particular research field, the practical consequences of his findings or maybe even personal conviction. The point is that the decision he ultimately takes is up to him. In statistical analysis one of the first questions he has to decide is what level of probability is acceptable for the rejection of the null hypothesis. The difficulties in making this decision are obvious and in much educational research literature they are not really faced at all. What a large number of writers do is simply present the significance levels of the statistics they have computed. Thus you will often see such results as $r = 0.45 (p < 0.001)$, $r = 0.26 (p < 0.05)$. In fact the table of results presented in research papers often contain a column in which significance levels for each result are stated. Haddon and Lytton's table, which we saw in section 1 (Table 1), is a typical example.

7.3 But choosing a significance level is only the first step in statistical decision making. What about the tests themselves? Here we are faced with many more problems. The theoretical probability distributions on which statistical tests are based all rely for their existence on the notion of a random sample of observations of variables from a population for which certain assumptions can be made about the distribution of the variables and their parameters. Furthermore, as we have seen, each particular test relies on certain assumptions about the nature of the data we are dealing with. (You will find detailed discussions of these in most statistical textbooks.)

7.4 How far we can violate the assumptions on which a statistical test is based and still arrive at meaningful conclusions has bothered many people. We referred to the flight into non-parametric statistics as one example of perhaps a panic reaction to this problem. In some cases we have decision rules, such as those we saw in the chi-squared test, which are fairly easy to abide by. But in others we are on less certain ground. The majority of research reports you are likely to encounter for example make no pretence at having based their observations on samples drawn by random methods. Does this mean we should discount their findings? Furthermore the only source of error we have considered in statistical tests is sampling error. If we are dealing with unreliable measurements, such as in attitude research for example, then we have another source of error to contend with. As statistical tests take no account of this source of error, should we discount research findings for variables whose measurements have low reliability?

7.5 The answer to these questions is probably no. Any set of sample data is *one* of the possible random samples that could have been selected from a population. And the possibility of high measurement error in some research data can be seen simply as justifying the generally adopted practice of opting for high levels of statistical significance. However despite this reassurance we cannot avoid the fact that most data gives at best only a partial fit to our statistical probability models. It is also the case that the larger the sample we use, the more likely we are to find statistically significant results, regardless of whether they are of any real importance. The message which comes from this is to avoid putting all one's hopes on one significance test, but to rely much more on replicating it. If we have only limited opportunities to test a hypothesis then commonsense dictates that our findings need to be substantial in order to convince others.

7.6 *Summary* Any piece of reasonably designed research may play a part in contributing to our body of knowledge. What we have to do in evaluating it, therefore, is to try to weigh up the usefulness of its findings against the weaknesses in its design and analysis. The question is one of the confidence that we can place in a research conclusion. Any evidence is better than no evidence. But some types of evidence are very much better than others.

Objectives

By the time you have completed this Part of the Block you should be able to:

1   Understand the logic underlying the testing of statistical hypotheses.

2   Distinguish the two types of error in statistical decisions.

3   Understand the concept of the sampling distribution of a statistic and define the standard error.

4   Decide in which research situations a one-tailed test should be used instead of a two-tailed one.

5   Apply statistical tests to the difference of mean scores of two large samples on a variable.

6   Test the statistical significance of a correlation coefficient.

7   Test hypotheses concerning the difference between means on a variable for two small samples.

8   Test hypotheses concerning data in the form of contingency tables.

Answers to Self-assessment Questions

SAQ 1
The disadvantage would be that you would lose a great deal of information by dichotomizing. Some information about the distribution of scores is lost even by taking the mean as our measure, but a great deal more is lost when we treat every score as having effectively only two possible values ('high' or 'low').

SAQ 2
The completed table should look like this:

Table 14   Indications of statistical significance

Level	Probability limits	Frequency of a chance occurrence	Significance levels	Odds against a chance occurrence
Low	$p < 0.05$	5 in 100	5%	19 : 1
↓	$p < 0.01$	1 in 100	1%	99 : 1
High	$p < 0.001$	1 in 1000	0.1%	999 : 1

SAQ 3
(a)   Your original question is that involving parents in the life of the school improves children's attainment. You are treating a measure of reading attainment – a test score, say – as the operationalized measure of attainment, and the presence or absence of a PTA as the operationalized measure of involvement. Your research hypothesis would then be: 'Children in schools with PTAs will show a higher mean reading score than other children'. Alternatively, we might dichotomize reading scores at the overall median and say that: 'A higher percentage of the children in PTA schools will have reading scores above the overall median' – the d-statistic encountered in Part 2.

The null hypothesis in either case would be: 'The children in PTA schools do not differ from others with respect to reading scores'.

(b)   Given the *number* of PTA meetings, a slightly more sophisticated research hypothesis would be possible: 'Mean reading score is associated with number of PTA meetings'; or 'There will be a significant correlation between number of PTA meetings in a school and the mean reading score of its children'. The null hypothesis would be: 'Number of PTA meetings does not correlate with mean reading score'.

However, it would be possible for the *number* of PTA meetings to have no effect on the score but for the *presence* or *absence* of a PTA to influence attainment. A better design would be:

Research hypothesis	Null hypothesis
1 Schools with PTAs will show higher mean scores	They will not
2 In schools with PTAs (i.e. ignoring non-PTA schools) number of PTA meetings will correlate with mean score	It will not

SAQ 4

(a)   In this case, you are under pressure from both sides. On the one hand, you are advising the expenditure of a large amount of money if you reject the null hypothesis, so that finding an apparently real effect of the computer system on accidents where in fact no effect existed could be a very expensive mistake. On the other hand, your mistakes in rejecting a system which actually reduced accidents may be measured in avoidable deaths and avoidable injuries. You might well be inclined to set a fairly low significance level but one which is reasonably sure to reject the most obvious artefacts – the five per cent level, say. Even then, if your results were non-significant but not by much you might be inclined to run your experiment again on a larger sample or to design a more sensitive (*powerful*) experiment.

(b)   In this case, as a social scientist, the costs are unequally weighted. Presumably you would have to show that the new system is better than the old one, and to show it with a fair degree of certainty, before the potential customer is justified in replacing his old equipment. You would therefore presumably opt for a high significance level (one per cent, say) and a two-tailed test. (Who knows? The new equipment might even be worse than the old.) The manufacturer, on the other hand, might well be trying to pressurize you into using a low significance level and a one-tailed test; from his point of view, if the new equipment is no worse than the old he is justified in selling it.

(c)   In this case, the decision is a less vital and a less problematic one. Much of the ability to understand statistics is contributed by the students and the amount of work that they put into the course; your teaching materials only offer to help them and if the new ones were only a little worse than the old ones the effects would probably not be catastrophic. Indeed, if your new method is *developed* you can probably be confident that it will be at least no worse than the old one. You would probably opt for the five per cent significance level and this might even be a valid opportunity for a directional hypothesis and a one-tailed test.

SAQ 5

The table gives a probability of 0.0013 (0.13 per cent) associated with a z value of 3. However, this is the probability of finding a deviation as extreme as 3 *in one direction* (i.e. the one-tailed probability). To find the probability of a deviation that extreme *in either direction* (the two-tailed probability) we must multiply the table entry by two, giving a result of 0.0026 (0.26 per cent). In other words, a sample with this extreme a score should be found only 26 times in 10 000 (i.e. once in every 385 samples drawn, or virtually never).

SAQ 6

Difference in means $= 15.5 - 15.0 = 0.5$
Standard deviation $= 2$, with a sample of 101

Estimated standard error

$$= \frac{2}{\sqrt{100}} = \frac{2}{10} = 0.2$$

$$z = \frac{0.5}{0.2} = 2.5$$

The critical values at the 0.01 level are 2.58 for a two-tailed test and 2.33 for a one-tailed test. Therefore we can certainly reject a directional null hypothesis, but at this level of significance we cannot reject a non-directional one.

SAQ 7

Collapsing the table at the median, we get:

Table 15

Income	Borough 1	Borough 2	Total
$\leqslant$ £5 000	800	700	1 500
£5 001 +	200	1 300	1 500
$\leqslant$ £5 000	80%	35%	50%
£5 001 +	20%	65%	50%

$d = 45$ per cent (0.45, as a proportion).

$$s_d = \sqrt{p_c q_c \left(\frac{1}{n_1} + \frac{1}{n_2} \right)}$$

$$= \sqrt{0.50 \times 0.50 \times \left(\frac{1}{1\,000} + \frac{1}{2\,000} \right)}$$

$$= 0.0194$$

$$z = \frac{0.45}{0.0194} = 23.22$$

which is obviously significant even at the 0.001 level.

However, note that this comparison does not tell the whole story: although Borough 2 is richer on average as the full table shows, it actually has many *more* people in the bottom income category than Borough 1.

SAQ 8

$$s_r = \frac{1}{\sqrt{50}} = 0.1414$$

Table 16

Variable (row)	Correlation	z	Significant? (two-tailed)
1	0.08	0.57	No
2	0.26	1.84	No
3	0.35	2.48	Yes
4	0.07	0.50	No
5	0.18	1.27	No
6	0.30	2.12	Yes
7	0.06	0.42	No
8	-0.41	2.90	Yes

SAQ 9

The standard error is given by

$$s_{d\bar{x}} = \sqrt{\frac{(n_1 - 1)s_{x_1}^2 + (n_2 - 1)s_{x_2}^2}{(n_1 + n_2 - 2)} \left(\frac{n_1 + n_2}{n_1 n_2}\right)}$$

$$= \sqrt{\frac{[12 \times (2.22)^2] + [17 \times (3.32)^2]}{(13 + 18 - 2)} \frac{(13 + 18)}{(13 \times 18)}}$$

$$= 1.0782$$

$$t = \frac{\bar{X}_1 - \bar{X}_2}{s_{d\bar{x}}} = \frac{6.0 - 8.33}{1.0782} = -2.16$$

with $13 + 18 - 2 = 29$ degrees of freedom. This is significant at the 0.05 level, so we can reject the null hypothesis.

SAQ 10

Expected values:

Table 17

Area	Via underpass	Via road	Total
A	41·41	71·59	113
B	20·16	34·84	55
C	8·43	14·57	23
Total	70	121	191

$$\chi^2 = \frac{(9.59)^2}{41.41} + \frac{(9.59)^2}{71.59} + \frac{(20.16)^2}{20.16} + \frac{(20.16)^2}{34.84} + \frac{(10.57)^2}{8.43} + \frac{(10.57)^2}{14.57}$$

$$= 56.252, \text{ with } (3 - 1)(2 - 1) = 2 \text{ degrees of freedom.}$$

With this size of table a χ^2 value of only 9.21 would be significant at the 0.01 level. We may therefore reject the null hypothesis decisively and conclude that use of the underpass is strongly affected by the nature of the area.

SAQ 11

Without Yates' correction, $\chi^2 = 7.00$. With it, $\chi^2 = 5.03$. There is one degree of freedom, so the critical values are 3.84 at the five per cent level and 6.64 at the one per cent level. At the five per cent level, therefore, we should have rejected the null hypothesis in either case. At the one per cent level, however, we might have rejected it if we had forgotten the correction, but we must accept it; that is, our hypothesis is not convincingly supported.

References

BYNNER, J. and STRIBLEY, K. M. (eds) (1979) *Social research: principles and procedures*, London, Longman/The Open University Press. (Course Reader.)

ENTWISTLE, N. J. and NISBET, J. (1972) *Educational research in action*, London, University of London Press.

GUILFORD, J. P. and FRUCHTER, B. (1973) *Fundamental statistics in psychology and education*, New York, McGraw-Hill.

HADDON, F. A. and LYTTON, H. (1968) 'Teaching approach and the development of divergent thinking abilities in primary schools', *British Journal of Educational Psychology*, Vol. 38, pp. 171–80.

HOFFMAN, L. R. (1958) 'Similarity of personality: a basis for interpersonal attraction?', *Sociometry*, Vol. 21, pp. 300–8.

KISH, L. (1959) 'Some statistical problems in research design', *American Sociological Review*, Vol. 24, pp. 328–38. Reprinted in Bynner, J. and Stribley, K. M. (eds) (1979) Ch. 8.

McNEMAR, Q. (1962) *Psychological statistics*, London, John Wiley.

POTTER, S. (1978) *Modal conflict at the mezzo scale*, Milton Keynes, The Open University, New Towns Study Unit.

SELVIN, H. C. and STUART, A. (1966) 'Data-dredging procedures in survey analysis', *American Statistician*, Vol. 20, pp. 20–3. Reprinted in Bynner, J. and Stribley, K. M. (eds) (1979) Ch. 21.

SIEGEL, S. (1956) *Non-parametric statistics for the behavioral sciences*, New York, McGraw-Hill.

Acknowledgements for Parts 1, 2 and 3

Grateful acknowledgement is made to the following for permission to reproduce material in this Block:

Part 1 *Figure 1* from S. MacIntyre, *Single and pregnant*, Croom Helm Ltd., 1977; Letter from *The Guardian* reproduced by permission.

Part 2 *Table 1 and Figure 1* from *Department of Employment Gazette*, May 1977, reproduced by permission of the Controller of HMSO; J. Goldthorpe for permission to use data from the Oxford Social Mobility Survey.

Part 3 *Table 11* from S. Potter, *Modal conflict at the mezzo-scale*, The Open University New Towns Study Unit, 1978.

Notes

Notes

DE304   Research Methods in Education and the Social Sciences

Block 1   VARIETY IN SOCIAL SCIENCE RESEARCH

Part 1	Styles of Research	M. J. Wilson
Part 2	How Research is Evaluated	John Bynner
Part 3	The Language of Social Science Research	M. J. Wilson

Block 2   BEGINNING RESEARCH

Part 1	Research Questions and Hypotheses	Martin Bulmer
Part 2	The Use of Secondary Sources	Martin Bulmer and Paul Atkinson
Part 3	Use and Interpretation of Published Statistics	Christopher Brook, Michael Drake, Robert Peacock, Andrew Pollard and R. J. Sapsford
Part 4	Descriptive Statistics	R. W. Lewis

Block 3   RESEARCH DESIGN

Part 1	Causation and Control	Jeff Evans
Part 2	Experimental Design	Judith Greene
Part 3	Design of Surveys	Betty Swift
Part 4	Introduction to Applied Sampling	Judith Calder
Part 5	Research Design in Ethnography	Paul Atkinson
Part 6	Evaluation of Research Designs	Jeff Evans

Block 4   DATA COLLECTION PROCEDURES

Part 1	The Nature of Data	John Bynner
Part 2	Methods and Strategies of Survey Research	A. N. Oppenheim
Part 3	Data Collection in Ethnographic Research	Martyn Hammersley

Block 5   CLASSIFICATION AND MEASUREMENT

Part 1	Description and Classification of Data	John Bynner
Part 2	Principles of Measurement	Desmond L. Nuttall
Part 3	Composite Measurement	John Bynner, David Romney and Adrian Thomas
Part 4	Evaluation of a Data Collection Method	David Romney

Block 6   MAKING SENSE OF DATA

Part 1	Analysing Ethnographic Data	Martyn Hammersley
Part 2	Two Variable Analysis	Cathie Marsh
Part 3	Hypothesis Testing	John Bynner, John Murphy and R. J. Sapsford

Block 7   MODELLING RELATIONSHIPS IN DATA

Part 1	An Introduction to the Linear Model	A. E. G. Pilliner and Peter Coxhead
Part 2	Extending the Linear Model	Peter Coxhead
Part 3	Causal Modelling	Liz Atkins

Block 8   EVALUATION OF RESEARCH
Authors R. J. Sapsford and Jeff Evans

Part 1	Evaluating a Research Report
Part 2	Planning Research
Part 3	Styles of Research Reconsidered

Block Co-ordinators

Block 1 M. J. Wilson, Block 2 Robert Peacock, Block 3 Jeff Evans and John Bynner, Block 4 John Bynner, Block 5 John Bynner, Block 6 M. J. Wilson, Block 7 Peter Coxhead and M. J. Wilson, Block 8 R. J. Sapsford